Civil War
GARMENTS, HISTORY, LEGENDS AND LORE

Written by
Gina Capaldi and Alan Rockman

GOOD APPLE
A Division of Frank Schaffer Publications

★ ★ ★ ★

With much gratitude and respect, I dedicate this book to
Douglas Rife and Kristin Eclov. Thank you for everything.
— G. C.

Senior Editor: Christine Hood
Editor: Concetta Doti Ryan, M.A.
Inside Design: Stephanie Villet Berman
Cover Design: Riley Wilkinson

 GOOD APPLE
A Division of Frank Schaffer Publications
23740 Hawthorne Boulevard
Torrance, CA 90505-5927

Contents

Introduction

In the early morning hours of April 12, 1861, Confederate General P. G. T. Beauregard opened fire on Fort Sumter. The only life lost was that of a Confederate horse. This was the beginning of a war that remains the bloodiest in American history. Why did so many men and women fight in a war in which struggle, crude weapons, and unfit conditions were the norm? Why were the North and the South so passionately divided?

In many ways, the immense force of the American Civil War still vibrates today. Political, constitutional, and human rights issues remain unresolved. During the Civil War, many of these issues became so complex that Northerners and Southerners were willing to die for their point of view rather than compromise. But after four long years, Johnny Reb and Billy Yank learned how similar they were to each other. The war grew old and it's meaning was all but lost.

In this book, students will discover many of the battles, personalities, and reasons for the war that forever shaped the history of our nation. Hands-on individual and group projects will expand students' understanding of the inventiveness exhibited during the Civil War, as well as the lifestyles of the Victorian era. This book offers students an experience that is vastly different from a textbook-based approach.

The activities in this book are intended to inspire a historical understanding of the Civil War, the people of the North and the South, and an overview of the 1800s. Many of these projects use today's materials, but we hope that efforts will be made to use materials that are as close to authentic as possible.

Suggestions for Using This Book

The information in this book may be used separately or in tandem with Civil War curriculum and U.S. history textbooks. The background information in each chapter is simplified to help children gain a better understanding of the basic concepts and actions which occurred during the Civil War. The legends and projects enhance individual and cooperative learning skills, while incorporating language arts, mathematics, critical thinking, and social studies content skills.

In each chapter you'll find . . .

• background information describing major events that changed the course of the Civil War.

• legends that have been documented as true—life experiences from the heroes of the day.

• reproducibles that show clothing, uniforms, accouterments, and sundries, all of which are specific to the era. Students may decorate these articles by following the color keys provided. They might also incorporate them into individual or group projects.

• step-by-step directions for group and individual projects based on the lifestyle of the era and the Civil War.

You also get . . .

• a large, colorful map indicating the various official and unofficial uniforms and accouterments used during this nation's Civil War. The placement of the uniformed figures indicates the general location where these troops originated. Also incorporated in the map are many inventions and articles of war that represent this time period.

• a bibliography listing a multitude of resources for you and your students to use for further research. This list includes children's literature references, activity books, Internet addresses, and general reference books.

How to Start

Begin by sharing the background information with your students. Show them the figures in their various uniforms and discuss how they differed from one army division to the next. Define which soldiers fought for the Confederate Army and which fought for the Union Army. Discuss how difficult, if not impossible, it would be to fight in a war in which everyone was dressed differently. Look at the artifacts, accouterments, and various sundries, and help students understand the simple life these men lived. Next, distribute copies of the reproducibles to each student. Share some of the following ideas by using the elements included on the reproducibles. Encourage your students to come up with their own ideas; after all, this was the Civil War era, a time of inventiveness in our country.

Basic Materials for Shadowbox and Limber-Jacks (pages 6 and 7)

– white posterboard
– scissors
– cardboard or oak tag
– tape recorder and tapes
– boot box or large shoe box
– poster paints (black, gold, red, purple, blue, and green)
– white glue
– velvet cloth, approximately 18" x 12" (45 cm x 30 cm)
– wood board, 2" (5 cm) wide by 3" (7.5 cm) long, and no more than 1/2" (1.25 cm) thick
– popsicle stick
– dowel, 3/8" (1 cm) wide
– six thumbtacks
– eight small cup hooks
– two small nails
– rubber bands
– hammer
– needle and thread or fabric tape
– pliers
– flashlight (optional)

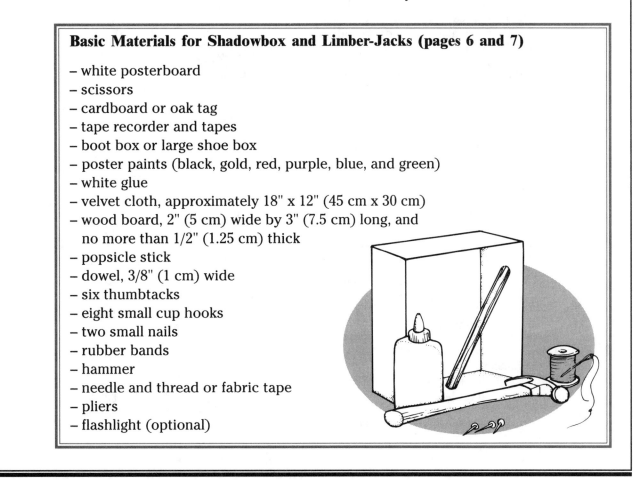

THEATER SHADOWBOX

During the war, men were known to put on performances in the camps. Many of these productions were the classics such as Shakespeare. Because only men served in the army, some were forced to play the female roles. This was all done in fun and out of boredom from the long months of inactivity. After the war, many heroes and spies, particularly women, took their "show on the road" and told their audiences of their exciting exploits. A week after the Civil War ended, President Lincoln went to Ford's Theatre, where he was assassinated.

1. Make a copy of President Lincoln (page 18) and mount on cardboard or oak tag. Leave a one-inch (2.5 cm) flap on the bottom and cut out the figure. Fold flap to make the figure stand upright. (Figure 1)

2. Cut the posterboard to fit around the top and sides of the boot box. Leave an extra three inches (7.5 cm) to make an overhang or facade around the top and sides. (Figure 2)

3. Enlarge a Victorian-type pattern and repeat it's design to cover the white posterboard facade. (Figure 3)

4. Paint the pattern using rich colors such as gold, red, purple, blue, and green. Allow to dry, then outline in black.

5. Use the needle and thread or fabric tape to hem the velvet with enough space to allow a dowel to slip through. (Figure 4)

6. Carefully cut two holes in the middle at the top of each side of the boot box. (Figure 5)

7. Slip the dowel rod with the velvet curtain on it into both holes of the box. (Figure 6)

8. Glue the facade to the shoe box. (Figure 7)

9. Record President Lincoln's famous Gettysburg Address, the Emancipation Proclamation, and the song "Battle Hymn of the Republic." Hide it and a tape recorder behind the box.

10. Glue the President Lincoln figure in the center of the box.

11. To add a dramatic effect to the speech, turn a flashlight on and point it toward the theater like a spotlight. Turn the classroom lights out, then turn the recorder on and listen to the speech.

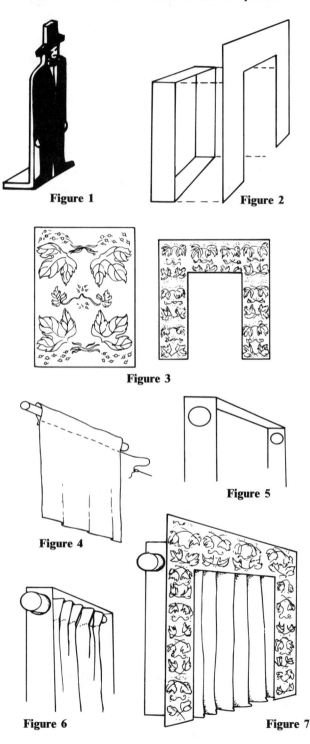

Figure 1

Figure 2

Figure 3

Figure 4

Figure 5

Figure 6

Figure 7

CIVIL WAR LIMBER-JACKS

Limber-jacks are traditional toys. They dance on a stick that is held from behind. This limber-jack may be used in conjunction with the Theater Shadowbox.

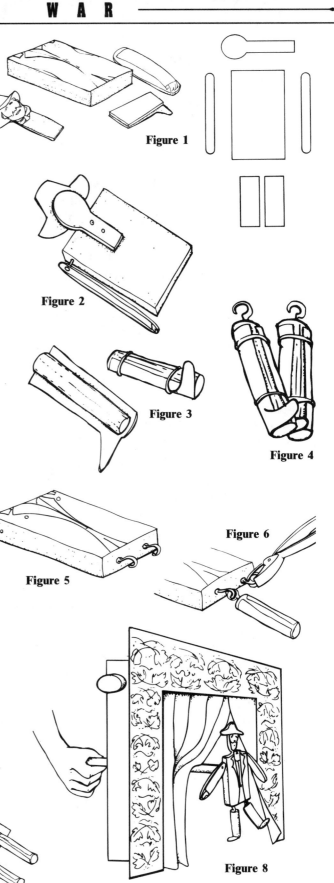

Figure 1

1. Copy the desired Civil War leader or soldier from this book, and color it by following the color key. Mount on lightweight posterboard.

2. Carefully cut out the head, arms, and legs. Draw the patterns on sturdy cardboard. Carefully cut out the head, arms, and legs from the form and glue to the patterns. Glue the body to the wood board. (Figure 1)

3. Tack the head form onto the wooden body. Nail the arms onto the sides. Make sure you keep the nails free from the body so that the arms swing freely. (Figure 2)

Figure 2

4. Cut two sections of the dowel about four inches (10 cm) for the length of the legs. Glue the legs onto the section. Use rubber bands to hold down the paper against the dowel while the glue is drying. (Figure 3)

Figure 3

Figure 4

5. Screw the cup hooks on top of the leg dowel. Follow the same process for the other leg and dowel. (Figure 4)

6. Screw the two remaining hooks into the lower part of the body where the legs will be. (Figure 5)

Figure 6

Figure 5

7. Close the hooks on the body with the pliers. Slip the top portion of the dowel hook for the legs into the body and close the hook. (Figure 6)

8. Center the remaining dowel in the back of the body and glue straight. (Figure 7)

9. Once Limber Jim has dried, move the stick back and forth and tap the legs on the ground to make him dance. Place the figure in the Shadowbox Theater with your arm behind the curtain. (Figure 8)

Figure 7

Figure 8

A DAY IN THE LIFE OF A CIVIL WAR SOLDIER

Living History Campsite Reenactment

Create a living history campsite in your classroom or school grounds. More often than not, the soldiers of the Civil War were "held up" in camp during the winter months. The remainder of the time, they set up small, makeshift camps that were easy to pack away for the next day's march.

While preparing for this project, students should study how soldiers lived and what they did while living in camp. Some of their activities included cooking, sewing, playing cards, reading, studying maps, sleeping, and writing letters. Each participant should be able to act out various chores or activities and be ready to answer any questions another student might ask about the period.

The first thing to decide is whether the camp is Confederate or Union. The common colors or the standard uniforms are Confederate gray or butternut and Union blue. Wearing student-crafted uniforms is not imperative, but it does make this project more authentic.

Basic Uniform

• Uniform coat

• Uniform pants—A strip running down the side of each outside pant leg will authenticate the look. Use one-half-inch wide (1.25-cm) yellow, white, or light blue upholstery tape for the Union, and red or white tape for the Rebels.

• Suspenders

• Felt cap or hat

• Shoes—Black Hush Puppies™ or boots will closely resemble what the soldiers wore.

• Wool socks

• Shirt—White with long sleeves for Union; white or plaid for Confederate.

• Belt—Black or brown leather with large brass buckles. Another look is using oversized pants held up with a rope. During the Civil War, oversized pants were not a fashion statement but a sad reminder of soldiers' malnourishment and starvation.

• There were hundreds of women who dressed as men during this time. Today, girls may choose to dress as the men or as a visiting wife or nurse. If this is the case, a long black or brown dress should be worn. Also, nurses often wore aprons.

Accouterments

- Canteen—If one is not available, take two regular-sized sturdy paper plates and tape them together (front to front). Paint with black or aluminum-colored paint. Cut a small hole in the top so a cork will fit as a stopper. Staple rope or a black strap to each side. (Figure 1)

- Haversack—Make a large canvas bag with straps. Cut a 3' x 1' (.9 m x .3 m) piece of canvas. Spray-paint both sides of the canvas. Use black for Union or tan for Confederate. Fold fabric over and sew both sides. Cut a 3' x 2" (.9 m x 5 cm) canvas strap. Paint it and attach its ends to the inside of the haversack. (Figure 2) Stuff the haversacks with sewing kits, combs, toothbrushes, cards, chess sets, glasses, candles, books, pencils, parchment paper, and so on.

- Cartridge box—Use or make a cardboard box that is six inches (15 cm) high, one and one-half inches (4 cm) wide, and four inches (10 cm) tall. Paint it black and attach the strap to both sides. (Figure 3)

- Eating utensils—Use tin plates and cups, forks, spoons, and knives. Spray-paint plastic utensils with silver paint. Do not use foam plates because aerosol paints can eat away the material.

- Cooking utensils—Old pots, frying pans, and spoons can be found at garage sales.

- Wool blanket—The more worn the better.

- Tent—Use two old white sheets sewn together. Use two tall sticks or old broom handles to hold the tent up. Two coffee cans filled with sand will hold the sticks in place as if they were imbedded in the ground. Rocks will help pull the tent skirting out. (Figure 4)

- Fireside—Use three tall sticks or old broom handles tied together in a tripod. Attach a tin pail or old (clean) paint can to a chain in the middle of the tripod. Old logs will help look as if it's fire wood. (Figure 5)

- Chairs—Old crates, wooden boxes or barrels, or tree stumps work well.

- Maps—Maps can be made to look worn by staining them with coffee or tea. Let them dry and then wrinkle them up to soften the paper. General Grant used pins to identify where troops were on the map. Students can mark the maps using toothpicks.

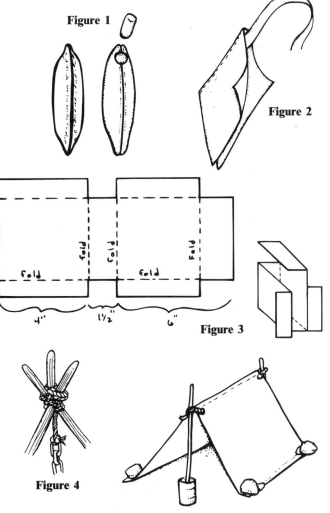

Figure 1

Figure 2

Figure 3

Figure 4

A House Divided

BACKGROUND INFORMATION

The years 1860 and 1861 were pivotal points in American history. At this time, the United States was still a growing country. There were only 34 states in the Union. The desire to settle new territories in the West seemed to drive the entire nation forward.

However, these times were also marked with heated political debates from both northern and southern statesmen. Representatives from both sides fought bitterly against each other. No amount of compromise was able to suppress the arguments. Political resentment grew and the "divided house" opened the door for the Civil War.

Most Americans had very little understanding of the tension within their government. Most worked on farms or lived in small towns that dotted the land between the eastern seaboard and the Mississippi River.

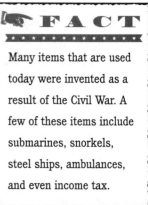

Lamp Used for Lincoln's Political Parades

Old Problems

Ever since the drafting of the Constitution in 1787, the Tenth Amendment, or "States Rights," remained an article of dispute. The Tenth Amendment states: "The powers not delegated to the United States by the Constitution, nor prohibited by it to the States, are reserved to the States respectfully, or to the people." The intent of this amendment was a result of the founding fathers' fear of giving the federal government too much power over individual states. The amount of federal power and control had never been established.

In the 1800s, the Tenth Amendment debates grew more complicated regarding federal control over the economy, taxes, and slavery. The northern statesmen wanted the federal government to have more power because of their political interests. They had enjoyed a strong economy due to their productive factories, seaports, and ship-building industries. On the other hand, the economy of the South relied solely on cotton. When tariffs or taxes were imposed on all states for western expansion, southerners argued that taxes were

Muzzle-loading muskets were used at the beginning of the war. More sophisticated weaponry was developed later.

FACT

Many items that are used today were invented as a result of the Civil War. A few of these items include submarines, snorkels, steel ships, ambulances, and even income tax.

too high. Higher taxes meant they would have to charge more for cotton in a competitive market. They also argued that the taxes only funded northern interests.

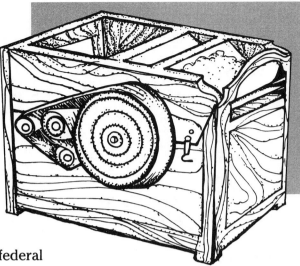

Historically, the South's economy had always suffered. However, after the invention of the cotton gin in 1792, there was an increased demand for slaves. Southern plantations began to flourish. But northern abolitionists reported the cruelty, family separations, and harsh lifestyles imposed on the southern slaves. By 1820, the abolitionists' movement put pressure on the federal government to abolish slavery. Federal law was passed to prohibit the expansion of slavery into the newly acquired "free states" of the Union, such as California. This new law was called the Missouri Compromise.

Cotton Gin

Southern statesmen knew that the free states would continue to grow through western expansion. They believed that the free states' representation in the government, along with the North, would out-number southern votes. The southerners felt that without slavery and equal representation, the South would be ruined.

A New President Is Elected

The presidential elections were held in 1860. The strong Democratic Party, which had always upheld southern interests, suddenly split in two. The split was a result of dissension between the southern radicals and conservatives. The radicals wanted to secede from the Union, while the conservatives did not feel it was in the best interest of the South to leave. Each side nominated its own candidate to run for the presidency. At the same time, the newly formed Republican Party nominated Abraham Lincoln as their candidate. Abraham Lincoln was known as a moderate repub-lican. It was hoped that his political position would heal the old wounds between the northern and southern statesmen. Radical southern extremists recognized that they could not win the presi-dential elections. South Carolina declared it would secede from the Union if Lincoln won.

On November 6, 1860, Lincoln won the election without a single southern vote. On December 20, 1861, South Carolina seceded from the Union. They declared themselves a separate and inde-pendent country having no allegiance to the North or the South. In early January, Alabama, Florida, and Mississippi also seceded. Soon after came Georgia, Louisiana, and Texas.

In November 1861, Jefferson Davis was voted the first president of the Southern Confederacy of America. Before the war, Davis had served as U.S. Senator for the state of Mississippi, and Secretary of War during President Franklin Pierce's adminis-tration. In May 1865, Davis was captured while fleeing from the Union Army. His citizenship was taken away and was not restored until 70 years later.

On February 8, 1861, representatives from the seven independent states met in Montgomery, Alabama. They proposed a new form of government called the Confederate States of America. Shortly after, the Confederate government ordered that every federal fort and building on southern soil be seized.

The War Begins

Abraham Lincoln was inaugurated as president on March 4, 1861. In his Inaugural Address, Lincoln tried to preserve the Union by assuring the South that he would respect their constitutional rights. He also pledged to the entire country that he would maintain control of all federal properties. This message made it clear to the Confederacy that Lincoln would stand against them if federal buildings continued to be seized.

The Confederate government was not pleased with Lincoln's position and took action against federal property. Off the coast of South Carolina stood Fort Sumter. This fort was commanded by the federal officer, Major Robert Anderson, and his small garrison of men. The Confederate rebels demanded that Major Anderson surrender or they would take the fort by force. Major Anderson refused and on April 12, 1861, at 4:30 A.M., Fort Sumter was bombed. After two days, Major Anderson was forced to surrender the fort. The Civil War had begun. Lincoln quickly called for 75,000 Union volunteers and declared a naval blockade of all southern ports. Arkansas, North Carolina, Tennessee, and Virginia reacted against the Union and seceded to join their southern brothers in their fight.

**Lottery Wheel
Used for Draft**

LEGEND

The Major's Wife Brings
Reinforcement to Fort Sumter

Just before the Civil War began, Major Anderson of the Federal Army was directed to take his small group of soldiers to Fort Sumter. But this made no sense to Mrs. Anderson, for her husband had only ten officers, 15 musicians, and 55 artillery men at his side—hardly an army to withstand the attacks from thousands of southern infantry troops.

Mrs. Anderson appealed to the government to send more men to the fort but was told it was impossible. Desperate to find someone to help her husband, Mrs. Anderson remembered a sergeant who served under her husband during the war with Mexico. This man, Peter Hart, had long proven himself to be a loyal and faithful soldier.

Together, Mrs. Anderson and Sergeant Hart traveled to South Carolina. She was terrified at what she saw—thousands of southern recruits hastening to join the Confederacy for a bloody attack. Mrs. Anderson immediately appealed to her father's old friend, the governor of South Carolina, to be allowed to see her husband. A pass was given to her to go to the fort, but Sergeant Hart's request was denied. Mrs. Anderson grew furious. "How is it that South Carolina would be endangered by one addition to a garrison of no more than 80 men? All the while you have thousands of men armed to fight them," she questioned. The governor saw how absurd his refusal was and gave the additional pass to Hart.

A small boat carried Mrs. Anderson and Sergeant Hart to Fort Sumter. Reaching the fort, Major Anderson grabbed his wife and hugged her. "I have brought you Peter Hart," she said. "The children are all well and I must leave tonight." Within two hours, Mrs. Anderson left her husband and his faithful friend behind.

She alone was able to get reinforcement through enemy lines, where the federal government could not.

GROUP PROJECT

Political Buttons

Presidential elections during the Civil War were handled much like they are today. Each political party chose members they believed would best represent their party platforms or views. During the presidential campaign in 1860, there were 33 states in the Union and four political parties.

Lincoln

NORTHERN CANDIDATES

ABRAHAM LINCOLN—REPUBLICAN PARTY
Platform: Free speech, free homes, and free territory. They also held that tariffs or taxes would be a benefit for businesses. They had no intention of interfering with slaveholders in areas that slavery was already accepted, but did oppose the expansion of slavery into free states and other territories.

STEPHEN A. DOUGLAS—NORTHERN DEMOCRAT
Platform: Believed that the settlers of the western territories needed to determine for themselves whether or not they wanted slavery. They believed in the preservation of the Union and programs built to suit the common man.

Douglas

Breckinridge

SOUTHERN CANDIDATES

JOHN C. BRECKINRIDGE—SOUTHERN DEMOCRAT
Platform: Pro-slavery but against the succession from the Union.

JOHN BELL—CONSTITUTIONAL UNION PARTY
Platform: Opposed northern and southern extremists and believed in the preservation of the Union.

Bell

Before You Begin

Have students choose a state and political candidate for whom to campaign. You might want to ask them where their ancestors lived during the 1860s. If they had families living in territories instead of states, help them establish how they might have voted given their state's location. Some students might have had families living outside the borders of the United States during this time. Divide this group between the northern and southern states.

Materials

- white glue
- silicone adhesive
  (found in drug and hardware stores)
- cardboard or sturdy manila folders
- scissors
- crayons or felt-tip pens
- safety pins
- red, white, and blue ribbons

Making Political Buttons

1. Enlarge each state or flag design to
   approximately three inches (7.5 cm).
   The designs are found on page 17.

2. Color the design by following the color key.

3. Enlarge the figures of the presidential candidates to
   three inches (7.5 cm), and color. Figures are located
   on page 14. (Figure 1)

4. Glue the state and candidate designs onto cardboard
   and cut out. Glue the candidate on top of the state
   design. (Figure 2)

5. Turn the button over and glue the pin onto the back
   of the button with silicone adhesive. (Figure 3)

6. Attach ribbons to back and let hang down. (Figure 4)

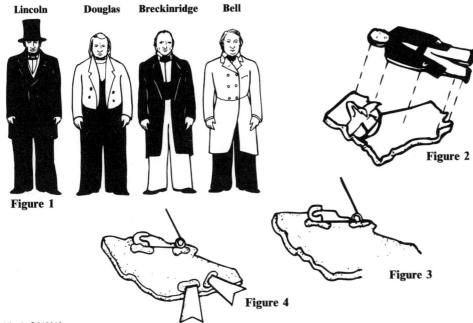

Lincoln   Douglas   Breckinridge   Bell

Figure 1

Figure 2

Figure 3

Figure 4

INDIVIDUAL PROJECT

Lincoln "Pasties"

"Pasties" were painted three-dimensional collages made before the Civil War. Many of these pasties represented favorite activities such as horseback riding. At the same time, most people were nationalistic and proud of their birth state. In this project, we celebrate Abraham Lincoln, 16th president of the United States, and his home state through a pastie design.

Materials

- 2 cups (500 mL) baking soda
- 1 cup (250 mL) cornstarch
- 1 1/4 cups (313 mL) water
- pot
- rolling pin
- flour
- scissors
- plastic knife
- white glue
- colored paper
- hair spray

Figure 1

Before You Begin

Enlarge the Illinois state or flag design to no more than 4 1/2" (11.25 cm). The design is located on page 17. Reproduce President Lincoln's shape from page 18.

1. Mix the baking soda, cornstarch, and water in a pot, and continually stir over a low heat. Once the mixture has thickened like mashed potatoes, set it aside to cool.

2. Sprinkle flour on the table and rolling pin. Roll out the clay mixture to 1/4" inch (.5 cm) thick.

Figure 2

3. Using the plastic knife, cut the clay material into a 6" x 6" (15 cm x 15 cm) square.

4. Lay the state or flag design in the middle of the square and incise or cut an impression of its outline. Let dry. (Figure 1)

5. Trace the state or flag design on the dry clay surface. Cut out colored paper to match the shape of the design, and glue. (Figure 2)

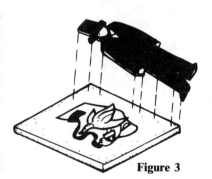

6. Cut President Lincoln out and glue him off to the side of the state or flag design. Spray with hair spray for a glossy sheen. (Figure 3)

Figure 3

Flag and State Designs

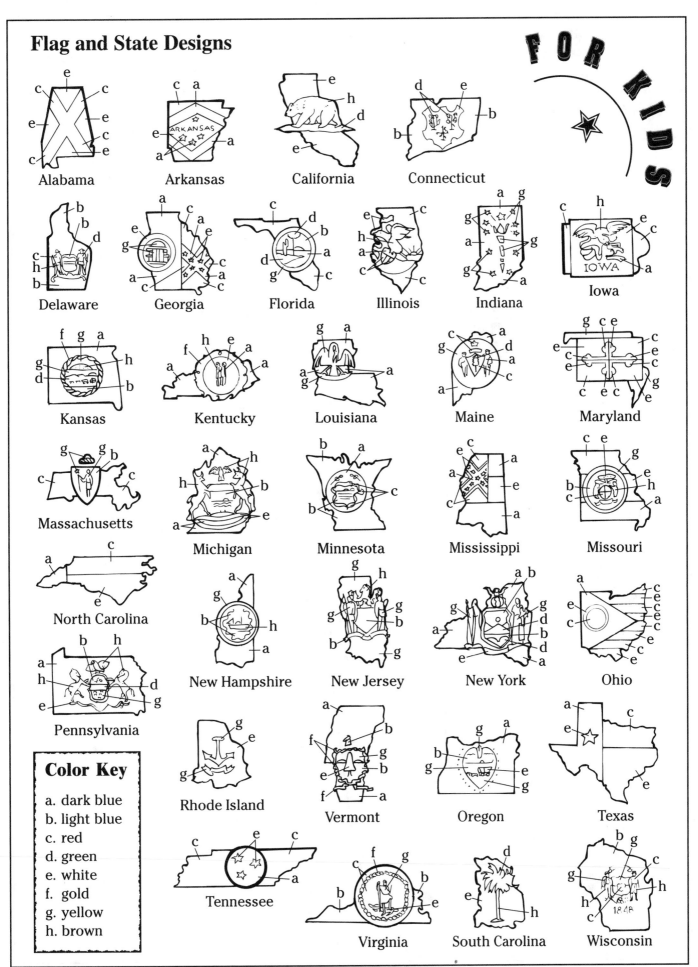

Color Key

a. dark blue
b. light blue
c. red
d. green
e. white
f. gold
g. yellow
h. brown

Alabama, Arkansas, California, Connecticut, Delaware, Georgia, Florida, Illinois, Indiana, Iowa, Kansas, Kentucky, Louisiana, Maine, Maryland, Massachusetts, Michigan, Minnesota, Mississippi, Missouri, North Carolina, New Hampshire, New Jersey, New York, Ohio, Pennsylvania, Rhode Island, Vermont, Oregon, Texas, Tennessee, Virginia, South Carolina, Wisconsin

Presidential Garments

Color the garments on President and Mrs. Lincoln by following the color key below.

Color Key

a. black
b. green
c. red
d. white
e. brown

Teacher's Note: Use this page as a flat coloring sheet or enlarge each item to use in one of the special projects described on page 6 or 14–16.

Lincoln Artifacts

Color the personal artifacts of President and Mrs. Lincoln following the color key below.

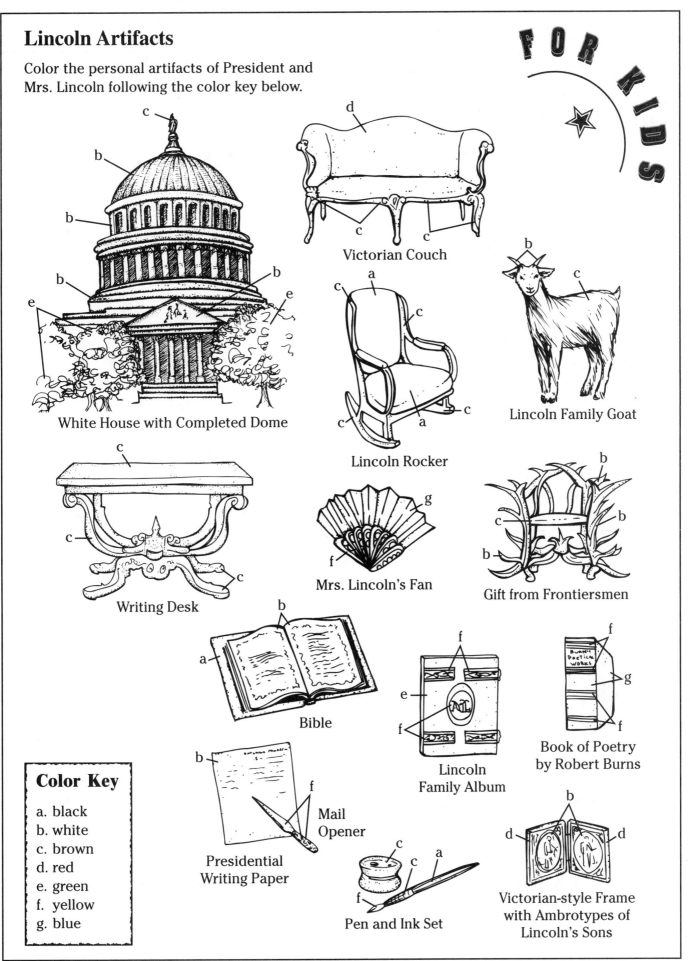

White House with Completed Dome

Victorian Couch

Lincoln Rocker

Lincoln Family Goat

Writing Desk

Mrs. Lincoln's Fan

Gift from Frontiersmen

Bible

Lincoln Family Album

Book of Poetry by Robert Burns

Presidential Writing Paper

Mail Opener

Pen and Ink Set

Victorian-style Frame with Ambrotypes of Lincoln's Sons

Color Key

a. black
b. white
c. brown
d. red
e. green
f. yellow
g. blue

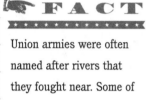

Rifle with Bayonet

The Making of the Volunteer Army

BACKGROUND INFORMATION

In the spring of 1861, patriotism was at an all-time high. Towns across the North and South held parades for the thousands of men who volunteered to fight in the nation's first Civil War. Northern politicians were confident that the Federal Army would crush the rebels and the war would end in one single battle. Southerners were convinced that protecting their constitutional rights and way of life was worth the fight.

A Call to Arms

President Lincoln originally offered Colonel Robert E. Lee the position as general in the Federal Army. Lee was a loyal Unionist until his beloved state of Virginia seceded from the Union. He felt such loyalty for his state that he followed. Shortly afterward, Lee left to become a respected general for the Confederate Army of Virginia. Major General Irwin McDowell was then appointed as the first general to command the federal troops in Washington, D.C.

For Federals and Confederates alike, the new civilian volunteers were in great need of discipline and training. Both armies had grown at such enormous rates that equipping them with uniforms and supplies was close to impossible. Many of the volunteers wore an odd assortment of uniforms furnished by individual state militias. Others wore uniforms outfitted by wealthy sponsors. Some soldiers wore their own civilian clothes. Unfortunately, many of the Rebel and Yankee uniforms were so similar that it caused dangerous confusion on the battlefield during the first battles of the war.

Weapons were another problem. The army-issued guns were in such limited supply that many of the first recruits used their own ancient muskets, pop guns, and even Bowie knives brought from home.

The First Major Battle

Fife

The capital of the Confederate States of America was centered in Richmond, Virginia, just 100 miles south of Washington, D.C. When the Rebel forces moved their troops into Richmond, northern citizens demanded that the Union Army take immediate action against the South.

General McDowell recognized that his volunteers had less than three months to prepare for war. Succumbing to political pressure, he moved his ill-fitted army across the Potomac River into Virginia. The men marched for days in the heat and dust. Their wool uniforms were miserable to wear. Many of the heavy backpacks, holding from 30 to 50 pounds of equipment, were quickly discarded.

On July 21, 1861, the Federal Army, 35,000 men strong, confronted 22,000 Rebel forces at Manassas Junction, Virginia—30 miles south of Washington D.C. The first major battle of the Civil War began near a little stream called Bull Run. The troops on both sides were spread out for miles. But the lack of discipline and training of both armies caused the men to fight in wild confusion. It was not long before a Federal retreat was sounded and the men stampeded back to their lines, dropping their weapons in a panic.

The Battle of Bull Run was a disastrous defeat for the Union Army, leaving 3,000 dead, wounded, or missing. The Rebels lost 2,000 men.

A Soldier's Life

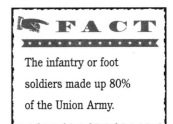

FACT

The infantry or foot soldiers made up 80% of the Union Army.

After the disaster at Bull Run, General McDowell was quickly replaced by Brigadier General George B. McClellan. He promised President Lincoln that he would transform the Union troops into disciplined soldiers. Each morning the men were awakened by a trumpet call. Then they spent hours marching and drilling. They learned to use their bayonets and rifles and pitch tents in the rain. The men also had a list of chores to keep them busy and organized. This list included repairing their equipment, tending horses, and building pathways and bridges. Many recruits grew frustrated with the daily camp routines and constant drilling. Their discontent grew worse as the weeks turned into months.

When the recruits were not drilling, they read; wrote loved ones; mended their clothes; and even organized bands, minstrel shows, and theater productions. They enjoyed playing chess, cards, or sports, but these games led into other less innocent activities such as drinking and gambling. Men were known to place bets on anything from cock fights to dice.

Food was plentiful in the first days of the war, but as time wore on, rations quickly became scarce. When food was available, it was tasteless or rotten. One such food was meat soaked in briny salt water. The soldiers called this meat "salt horse." In order to make the meat edible, the brine was scraped off, then soaked in water. The meat was fried in gobs of grease, which caused severe intestinal problems.

Hard Tack

Vegetables came in the form of dried cakes made of beans, carrots, beets, turnips, and onions. These "desecrated vegetables" were also known to have leaves and roots mixed among them. There were also crackers, or "hard tack," which were made with flour and water. These crackers were so hard and inedible that the soldiers called them "teeth dullers." More often than not, this staple was infested with weevils and maggots. The plight of the Confederate soldiers was no better. Their army supplied them with cornbread that quickly grew moldy.

Coffee was a favorite beverage for the Federal soldiers. Each man was given a ration of whole coffee beans. He pounded the beans with the butte of his rifle to grind them. The Confederate soldiers did not have this luxury. They made their beverages by boiling water with chicory, corn, and even peanuts they found.

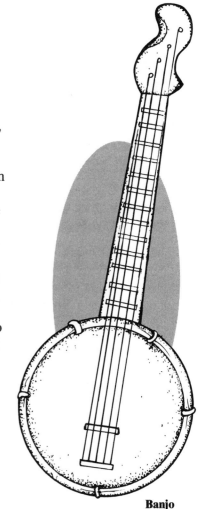

Banjo

LEGEND

General Beauregard and the Confederate Battle Flag

During the Battle of Manassas, Confederate General Pierre G. T. Beauregard peered through his looking glass. A body of troops moved in the distance. He grew anxious when he realized that he could not tell if these men were his own Confederate soldiers or the Federals. Their uniforms and the weapons that they carried were so similar it was almost impossible to tell them apart. The dust kicked up by the march covered everything and it was extremely difficult to see at a distance.

Time was running short and General Beauregard was desperate. He hoped that a gust of wind might open the distant troop's flag. He fixed his eyes on it. Was it the "Stars and Stripes" of the Federal Army or the "Stars and Bars" of the Confederates? He simply could not make it out. He enlisted the help of his soldiers but they, too, could not tell whose flag it was.

Time passed and the mysterious troop moved closer to the Federal lines. General Beauregard knew it would be a disaster if he let these Federal troops pass. But if they were Confederates and attacked them, it would be worse.

Suddenly, a puff of wind spread the flag open. Indeed, it was the Confederate flag—the Stars and Bars! General Beauregard sighed with relief. He vowed that his soldiers would have a new flag so distinct from the enemy that there would never again be any doubt.

After the Battle of Manassas at Bull Run, General Beauregard sought new battle flag designs. Many of them were created by Confederate wives. The first three battle flags of the Confederacy were made from ladies' dresses. The chosen design was presented to his troops. General Beauregard expressed that this new flag would be an emblem of victory and honor.

GROUP PROJECT

War Council "Colors," Flags, and Banners

Flags, or "colors," were a source of pride for the troops. During battles, these patriotic men responded to their flag and took great pains to carry it through battles—often at the expense of their own lives.

The first official flag, or "colors," for the Confederates was the "Stars and Bars." Unfortunately, it looked too similar to the Federal flag—the "Stars and Stripes." After the first battle of Manassas, a new Confederate flag was created. It was known as the Southern Cross. In it's design was a red field with two blue bands that crossed the middle. Inside the bands were 13 white stars that represented the 11 Confederate states. The two stars remaining were meant for Kentucky and Missouri who had yet to join the Confederate States of America.

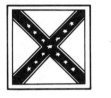

Materials

- closet rod or PVC pipe (for one project), 5 feet (1.5 m) tall
- four brass tacks (for one flag and pole)
- tape
- iron
- acrylic paints in assorted colors
- transfer paper
- fabric-fusing adhesive, 1/2" (1.25-cm) wide
- standard bucket or large plastic container to use for stand
- gray spray paint
- blue spray paint
- pen
- plaster
- fabric for standard flag 35" (87.5-cm) square (colors may vary depending upon design, please review page 27 for the color descriptions of the flags)

Before You Begin

Divide the class in half to represent the Union and Confederate states. Then, copy the flag and banner designs on page 27 and distribute them to students. From the designs, have students choose a specific design to reproduce. Discuss the importance of flags and banners as a source of pride, identification, and national heritage.

If Your Flag Has a Seal or Design

1. Prepare the closet rod for each flag by painting it blue for the Union or gray for the Confederacy. Let dry. Do the same for each bucket.

2. Some flags have an emblem or design. First, enlarge these designs with a copier. Tape the transfer paper onto the fabric. Lay the copied design into its position and follow the lines. (Figure 1)

3. Paint any details or outlines that are a part of the flag's design.

If Your Flag Has a Color Panel

4. Seal color panels together by folding the ends 1/2" (1.25 cm) at the edges. Place fusing adhesive between the two separate color panel edges and iron down. Make sure to read the manufacturer's directions before using the fusing material. (Figure 2)

Finishing Flags and Banners

5. Attach the flag to the appropriate colored closet rod pole with the brass tacks.

6. Mix the plaster as the instructions indicate, and pour it into the pail. Place the flag poles into the plaster for a display stand. (Figure 3)

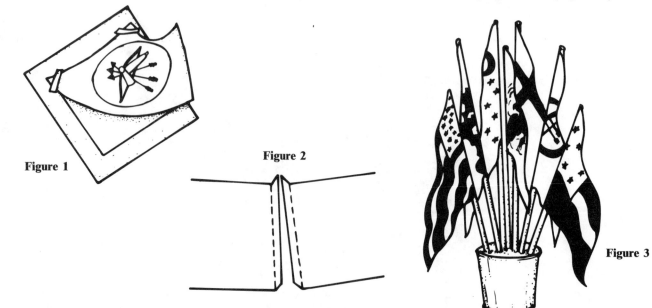

Figure 1

Figure 2

Figure 3

INDIVIDUAL PROJECT

Felt or Slouch Hats

Felt hats, or slouch hats, were popular during the 1800s. They had floppy brims and were worn by farm and country boys because they were easy to make and very sturdy. At the beginning of the war, many volunteers wore these hats.

Materials

- 6 ounces (185 mL) of pre-carded wool or combed wool (if carded wool is unavailable) You can find the wool in some craft stores.
- tape measure
- two plastic garbage bags or thin plastic bags
- 1 cup (250 mL) pure soap powder or flakes (not detergent) mixed with water
- rubber gloves
- scissors
- glass mixing bowl
- tarp
- spray starch or iron (optional)

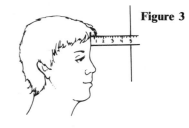

Figure 1

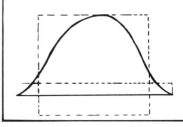

Figure 2

Figure 3

Making the Hat Pattern

1. You will need to make two bell-shaped patterns by using your head measurement. To find the width, measure around your head and divide the number by two. (Figure 1) Add an additional 2" for shrinkage.

2. To find the height, measure from the tip of your ear to the top of your head. Add 2" to that number. (Figure 2)

3. 4"–5" width is usual for the brim. Add 2" to that number for shrinkage. (Figure 3)

4. Take the measurements of the height, width, and brim and make two bell-shaped patterns. Draw these bell shapes onto the plastic. (Figure 4)

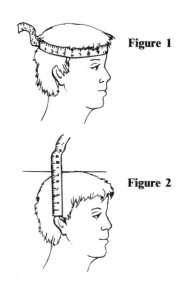

Figure 4

Layering the Wool and Felting

5. Place the first plastic pattern down on a tarp. Lay wool batts onto the pattern as if they were vertical shingles. Add an additional 1" seam of wool all around the edges, except the brim. (Figure 5)

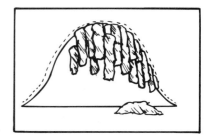

Figure 5

6. The second layer of wool should be shingled in a horizontal direction. (Figure 6)

7. Slip your hand under the plastic pattern and flip everything over. Be careful not to upset the layered wool. (Figure 7)

8. Pull the plastic pattern up and dribble some hot, soapy water into the middle of the wool. Lay the plastic back down and press to force the water through the wool fibers. Continue this process until all but the seam allowance is wet. (Figure 8)

9. Massage the wool fibers in small circular motions on the entire pattern for approximately 15 minutes. Do not change direction. If wool pulls apart, it is not yet felted. (Figure 9)

10. Fold the dry seam allowance over the back of the plastic. Set it aside. Follow the same process in steps 5 through 9 to make the second pattern of the hat.

11. Lay both felted sides together. Then, wet the seam allowances with the soapy water. Massage the seams together in small circular motion as you did with the rest of the hat. (Figure 10)

Fulling and Blocking the Hat

12. Once both sides of the hat have merged together, continue to rub it on a rough surface such as a washboard. It's okay to change direction during this process. Eventually the felt should become thick and stiff.

13. Try the hat on to see if it fits. Pull to adjust the size.

14. Rinse and squeeze out the soap and water. Set the hat on a table and let it dry. Press with an iron and a damp cloth or use spray starch to help stiffen the hat.

Figure 6

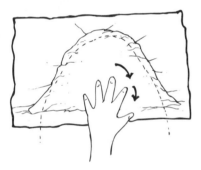

Figure 7

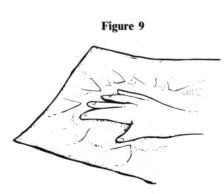

Figure 9

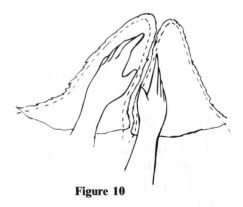

Figure 8

Figure 10

Flag Designs

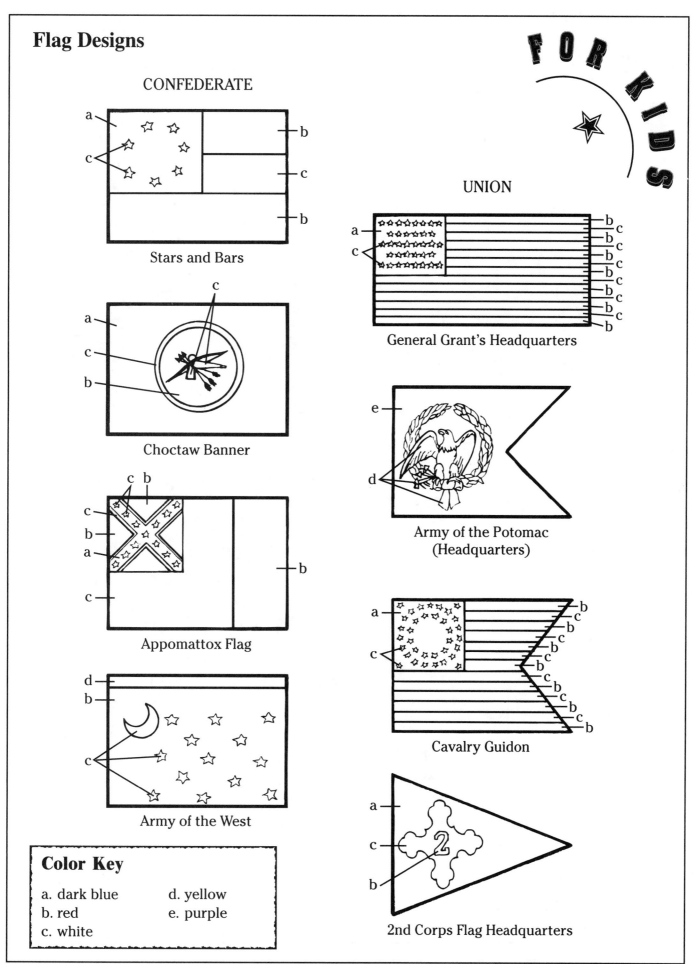

CONFEDERATE

Stars and Bars

Choctaw Banner

Appomattox Flag

Army of the West

UNION

General Grant's Headquarters

Army of the Potomac
(Headquarters)

Cavalry Guidon

2nd Corps Flag Headquarters

Color Key

a. dark blue   d. yellow
b. red   e. purple
c. white

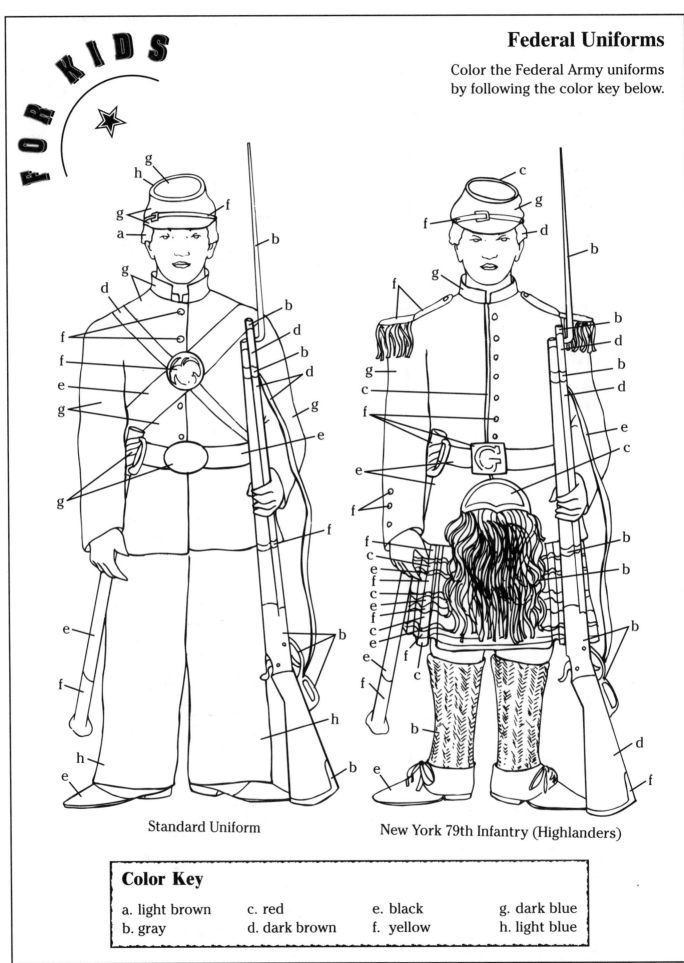

Federal Uniforms

Color the Federal Army uniforms by following the color key below.

Standard Uniform

New York 79th Infantry (Highlanders)

Color Key

| a. light brown | c. red | e. black | g. dark blue |
| b. gray | d. dark brown | f. yellow | h. light blue |

Union Sundries and Personal Affects

Color the Union soldiers' sundries and personal affects by following the color key below.

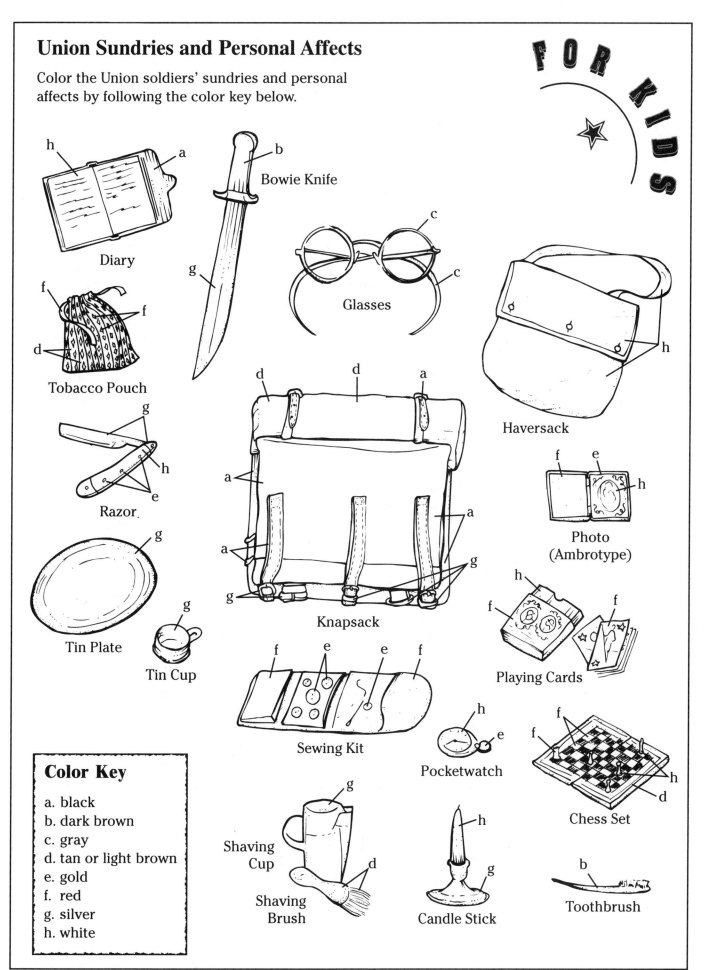

FOR KIDS

Diary

Bowie Knife

Glasses

Haversack

Tobacco Pouch

Razor

Tin Plate

Tin Cup

Knapsack

Photo (Ambrotype)

Playing Cards

Sewing Kit

Pocketwatch

Chess Set

Shaving Cup

Shaving Brush

Candle Stick

Toothbrush

Color Key

a. black
b. dark brown
c. gray
d. tan or light brown
e. gold
f. red
g. silver
h. white

Teacher's Note: Use this page as a flat coloring sheet.

29

The Widening War

BACKGROUND INFORMATION

The abolitionists, "colored troops," Native American Indians, immigrants, and women played vital roles in the Civil War. Some reached high acclaim, while others remained nameless. Their roles during the Civil War were none-the-less significant.

The Abolitionists

In 1820, the Missouri Compromise was passed. This new law kept slavery from becoming legal in certain territories and states. But abolitionists such as William Lloyd Garrison, Elijah Lovejoy, Henry Ward Beecher, and John Brown wanted slavery to be outlawed completely. The brave fugitive slaves, Harriet Tubman, Sojourner Truth, and Frederick Douglass, gave first-hand accounts of its brutality and dedicated their lives to winning freedom for their people. These abolitionists joined together to preach, write, and even publish newspapers in order to educate others against this southern institution.

Abolitionists also helped runaway slaves to freedom by secretly smuggling them to the northern states and Canada. They accomplished this through the underground railroad. Although not a railroad, many terms were used to cloak the real intent of this operation. Hidden routes to freedom were called "lines," the runaway slave was sometimes known as "freight," or a "passenger," and the stopping locations were called "depots" or "stations." Moving from one safe house to the next was referred to as "catching the next train." Those who helped the slaves reach their destinations were called "conductors." The underground railroad operated in 14 northern states. But the heaviest concentrations were in the states closest to the Canadian border.

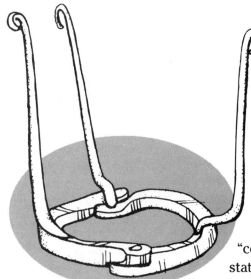

Slave's Pronged Collar

"Colored Troops"

At the beginning of the war, leading abolitionists urged President Lincoln to use black, or "colored," men in the Federal Army. However, even in the North, most soldiers refused to fight alongside black men. The majority of politicians also opposed this idea, as they believed it would lead to rebellion among the Union ranks. However, in 1863, Lincoln delivered his Emancipation Proclamation, which opened the way for Lincoln to authorize enlistment of black soldiers.

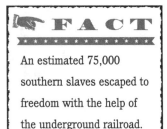

More than 186,000 black men fought for the Union Army. The colored troops faced more discrimination than any other group. They were first assigned hard labor that entailed long hours of menial work such as cleaning latrines and building roads. When they were finally able to participate in battles, they fought bravely and gained the respect of many officers.

The Confederate Army originally did not allow blacks to fight in the war. But in 1865, the Rebels became so desperate for manpower that they called for their own 300,000 black recruits. The "colored" units were organized in Richmond, Virginia. When the proud colored troops paraded in the streets, southern crowds flung stones and mud at them. The colored troops never had a chance to fight for the South because the war soon ended.

**Slave's
Wooden Carving**

FACT

Harriet Beecher Stowe, sister of famed abolitionist Henry Ward Beecher, wrote the classic novel *Uncle Tom's Cabin: Life Among the Lowly*. This novel was written as a statement against slavery, and in it's first week of publication, 10,000 copies were sold.

Foreign Forces

Many immigrants came to the United States to escape the poverty and oppression of their own countries. The United States offered them the opportunity for new jobs, land, and better futures. When the war broke out, half a million immigrant men volunteered for the North. They were subjected to mistreatment and ridicule by their native born counterparts. Even so, the foreign recruits fought hard for their adopted country.

The greatest number of foreign recruits on both sides were the Germans. Following them were the Irish. However, there were a multitude of other nationalities such as English, Dutch, French, Italians, Hungarians, Scandinavians, Scots, Spaniards, Poles, Russians, Jews, Mexicans, and Asians who also fought in the war.

FACT

The Union marching song, "Battle Hymn of the Republic," was written by a New York socialite, Julia Ward Howe. Writer Louisa May Alcott and poet Walt Whitman both served as nurses in the Civil War.

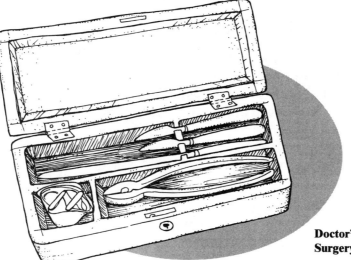

**Doctor's
Surgery Case**

Native American Indians

Although distrustful of the "white man's war," as many as 12,000 Native Americans served for the Confederacy. They had reputations for being strong fighters, but many never adapted to military life and its restrictions. Others refused to wear the standardized uniforms and opted to wear their own regalia, use war paint, and fight with their own weapons of bows and arrows.

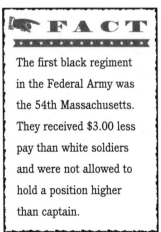

One noteworthy Native American Indian who committed his full allegiance to the southern cause was Stand Watie. Watie was a Cherokee leader who served as a general in the Confederate Army. Aside from fighting in several important battles west of the Mississippi, Watie was the last Confederate general to surrender his arms in June, 1865. The highest ranking Native American to serve in the Union Army was Ely S. Parker, an Iroquois from New York. He served as General Grant's private secretary and was present at Lee's surrender in Appomattox.

Prosthetic and Saw

FACT

Foreign royalty also fought for the cause. Prussian Prince Felix Salm-Salm served as a chief of staff in the Federal Army. There were also Swedish-born barons and Austrian counts who served. A French prince commanded in the South.

Women

With most of the men off at war, it became necessary for women to fill their positions at home. Women became farmers, shopkeepers, factory workers, and clerks. Others served by working in weapons plants. Hundreds of woman dressed like men and participated in the battles. Some of the most notorious spies were women. But the average woman participated in political fundraisers by sewing quilts or selling baked goods.

Dr. Elizabeth Blackwell organized women's relief efforts, which became the U.S. Sanitary Commission. This opened the door for thousands of women to serve as nurses in the Union Army. A few months later, Dorothea Dix was officially appointed Superintendent of Army Nurses for the Federal War Department. As the war continued, the call for dedicated nurses became great. Women like Clara Barton for the Union and Sally Tompkins for the Confederates, faced the filth, blood, cries, and death of the soldiers. These "angels on the battlefield" came to the aid of Rebel and Yankee soldiers alike.

FACT

The first black regiment in the Federal Army was the 54th Massachusetts. They received $3.00 less pay than white soldiers and were not allowed to hold a position higher than captain.

LEGEND

Harriet Tubman: The Moses of Her People

Even as a child, Harriet Tubman knew the injustice of slavery. No matter how hard she and the other slaves worked, they were still beaten. When her master died, Harriet learned she would be sold into the deep South. This meant that she would never again see her family and friends. Harriet had nothing to lose, so she took a chance and fled to freedom. Harriet's first experience with the underground railroad began.

Her first stop was at an obscure farm. The agents from the underground railroad handed her a broom and told her to sweep the yard. Passersby believed that Harriet belonged to the farm. In the evening, the farmer hid Harriet in a wagon. He tossed old quilts over her and filled the rest of the wagon with produce. Then, the long trek into the early morning hours began.

While traveling in secrecy with the underground railroad, Harriet covered 90 miles of unfamiliar terrain until she reached Pennsylvania. She slept on the ground; hid in haystacks, potato holes, and attics; and was rowed up and down rivers by people she had never met before. But when she found freedom, it was glorious! Harriet was determined that her loved ones would have the same freedom. She volunteered her own services to help in the underground railroad. Like many of the "conductors" and "agents," Harriet learned to be brave, daring, and cunning to bring her charges out safely. She became so good at being a conductor that slave owners were constantly on the lookout for her. Large rewards were offered, but she was never caught. Over 300 slaves were freed from bondage because of Harriet's own daring escapes.

When the Civil War began, Harriet volunteered as a nurse, scout, and sometimes even a spy.

GROUP PROJECT

Underground Railroad Story Quilts

Quilts are a part of American history. Since women were not allowed to vote, many voiced their opinions with quilt designs. The abolitionists sold hand-made quilts to support their anti-slavery cause. Those abolitionists who worked as agents in the underground railroad designed their quilts with secret messages. One design was the "log cabin." Originally, this design had a yellow center to symbolize the hearth or fireplace. But when the yellow center was replaced with a black center and the quilt was hung outside, it signaled that the house was a "safe house" for runaway slaves.

Before You Begin

Make enough copies of the quilt designs on page 37. Then, read the legend in this chapter on Harriet Tubman. Discuss the dangers and perils that runaway slaves would encounter as they made their way toward freedom. Use the following examples to show some of the ways agents in the underground railroad secretly helped runaway slaves. Have students create their own story lines as agents of the underground railroad or runaway slaves. Below are some symbols students may want to incorporate as they develop their story lines.

SAFE HOUSE—Any house where runaways could hide to be safe. One such "safe house" had a chimney with a circle of white bricks at the top.

TAPPING STONES—Soft tapping of stones was a signal to the runaway slave that it was safe to cross an exposed area.

LIGHTS—A blue light above a yellow light signaled an awaiting raft for runaway slaves.

SECRET CHAMBERS AND ROOMS—These secret hideaways included attics with false walls, secret closets, false cupboards, hidden doors that led to cellars, haystacks, wooded areas, barn floors, and church belfries, to name a few.

Materials

- assorted fabric scraps (upholstery fabric, corduroy, and velvet are beautiful but sometimes difficult to work with)
- fabric-fusing materials
- fabric scissors
- transfer paper
- tape
- pencil

- iron and ironing board
- one fabric square per child 6 1/2" x 6 1/2" (16.25 cm x 16.25 cm), muslin or cotton/polyester fabric
- straight pins
- two pieces of fabric for front and back, each 34" x 47" (85 cm x 117.5 cm)
- batting, 32" x 45" (80 cm x 112.5 cm)

Optional: Instead of a quilt made of fabric, use colored paper for the appliqués and butcher paper for the base fabric.

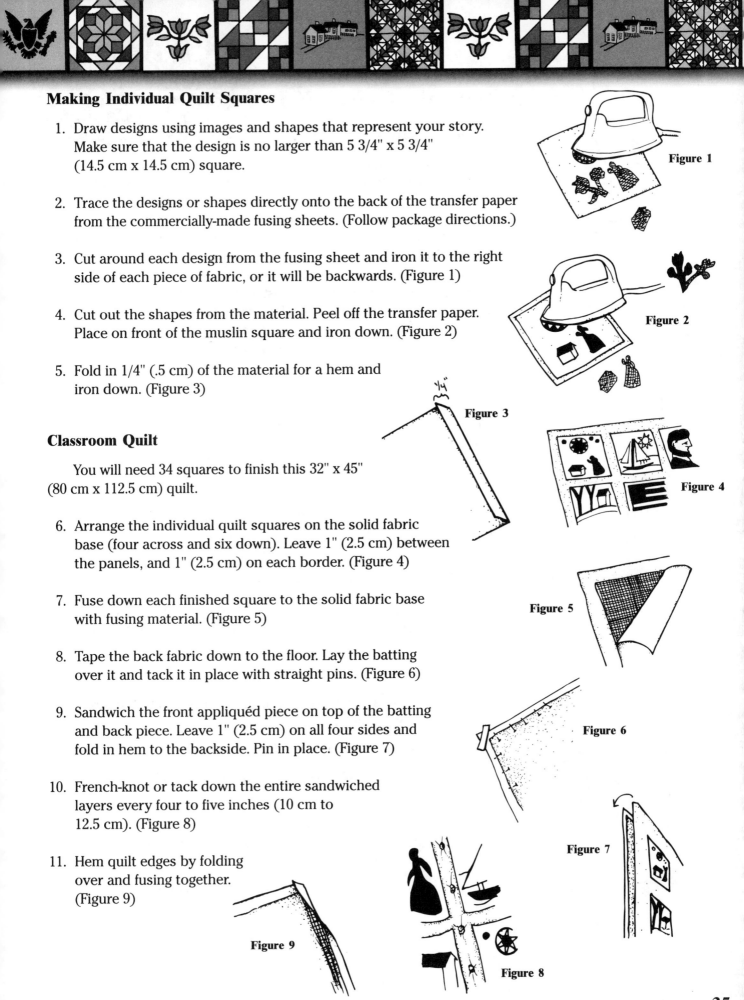

Making Individual Quilt Squares

1. Draw designs using images and shapes that represent your story. Make sure that the design is no larger than 5 3/4" x 5 3/4" (14.5 cm x 14.5 cm) square.

2. Trace the designs or shapes directly onto the back of the transfer paper from the commercially-made fusing sheets. (Follow package directions.)

3. Cut around each design from the fusing sheet and iron it to the right side of each piece of fabric, or it will be backwards. (Figure 1)

4. Cut out the shapes from the material. Peel off the transfer paper. Place on front of the muslin square and iron down. (Figure 2)

5. Fold in 1/4" (.5 cm) of the material for a hem and iron down. (Figure 3)

Figure 1

Figure 2

Figure 3

Classroom Quilt

You will need 34 squares to finish this 32" x 45" (80 cm x 112.5 cm) quilt.

6. Arrange the individual quilt squares on the solid fabric base (four across and six down). Leave 1" (2.5 cm) between the panels, and 1" (2.5 cm) on each border. (Figure 4)

7. Fuse down each finished square to the solid fabric base with fusing material. (Figure 5)

8. Tape the back fabric down to the floor. Lay the batting over it and tack it in place with straight pins. (Figure 6)

9. Sandwich the front appliquéd piece on top of the batting and back piece. Leave 1" (2.5 cm) on all four sides and fold in hem to the backside. Pin in place. (Figure 7)

10. French-knot or tack down the entire sandwiched layers every four to five inches (10 cm to 12.5 cm). (Figure 8)

11. Hem quilt edges by folding over and fusing together. (Figure 9)

Figure 4

Figure 5

Figure 6

Figure 7

Figure 8

Figure 9

INDIVIDUAL PROJECT

Victorian Hairwork Brooch

Making hairwork jewelry became a common pastime for Victorian women. The jewelry was worn as an expression of love and was made of the person's hair or that of a deceased loved one. Hairwork jewelry was common and used in everything from bracelets, earrings, and chokers to rings. The hair was prepared by boiling it in soda water for 15 minutes. Hair was sorted into 20 or more strands. Then, they were woven into patterns. Small gold joints and fittings were then added.

Gutta-Percha was a popular substance used for making jewelry in the Victorian era. This material came from tree sap and bogs. When it was heated and treated like rubber, it turned into a hard, natural plastic material. Because of its dark color, Gutta-Percha was used in mourning jewelry.

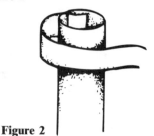

Figure 1

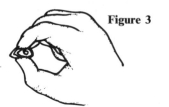

Figure 2

Materials

- brown or black paper strips, 1/8" (.25 cm) wide and varying lengths
- plastic glue
- cocktail straws
- scissors
- shellac or hair spray
- brown or black polymer clay, enough to make a 3" (7.5 cm) oval, 1/8" (.25 cm) thick

- safety pin
- silicone adhesive
- brown or black embroidery thread (should be the same color as paper quills)
- small picture of family member or friend (optional)

Figure 3

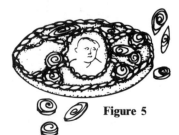

Figure 4

Figure 5

1. To make the base like a Gutta-Percha, mold the polymer clay into an oval 3" (7.5 cm) long, 1" (2.5 cm) wide, and 1/4" (.5 cm) thick. Let dry.

2. Using scissors, make two slits about 1/4" (.5 cm) deep in the top of the straw. (Figure 1)

3. Slot one end of your paper strip into the slits and wind the strip around and around the straw. (Figure 2)

4. Make your quilled paper into any shapes by squeezing them. (Figure 3)

5. Cut three strands of embroidery thread 10" (25 cm) long. Knot tightly at one end and braid.

6. If you are using a picture, glue it in the center of the brooch base. Then, glue the braided thread in swirling designs around the edges of the picture and around the base. (Figure 4)

7. Glue the paper quills inside the brooch frame. (Figure 5) Once the glue has dried, spray with clear shellac or hair spray.

8. Glue the safety pin to the back of the brooch with adhesive.

Quilt Designs

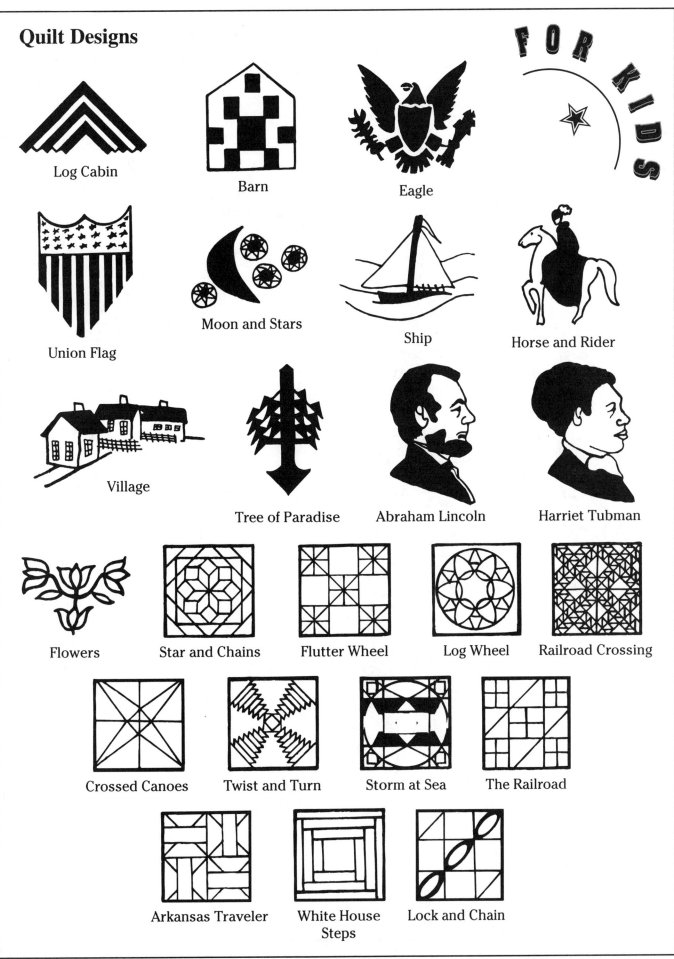

FOR KIDS

Log Cabin

Barn

Eagle

Union Flag

Moon and Stars

Ship

Horse and Rider

Village

Tree of Paradise

Abraham Lincoln

Harriet Tubman

Flowers

Star and Chains

Flutter Wheel

Log Wheel

Railroad Crossing

Crossed Canoes

Twist and Turn

Storm at Sea

The Railroad

Arkansas Traveler

White House Steps

Lock and Chain

Teacher's Note: Use this page as a flat coloring sheet or enlarge each item to use in one of the special projects described on pages 34–35.

© Good Apple GA13010

37

Union and Confederate Uniforms

Color the Union and Confederate uniforms by following the color key below.

56th Colored Infantry
(Union)

1st Cherokee Mounted Rifles
(Confederate)

Color Key

a. light blue	c. black	e. red	g. yellow
b. dark blue	d. brown	f. tan	

Teacher's Note: Use this page as a flat coloring sheet.

Confederate Sundries and Personal Affects

Color each item by following the color key below.

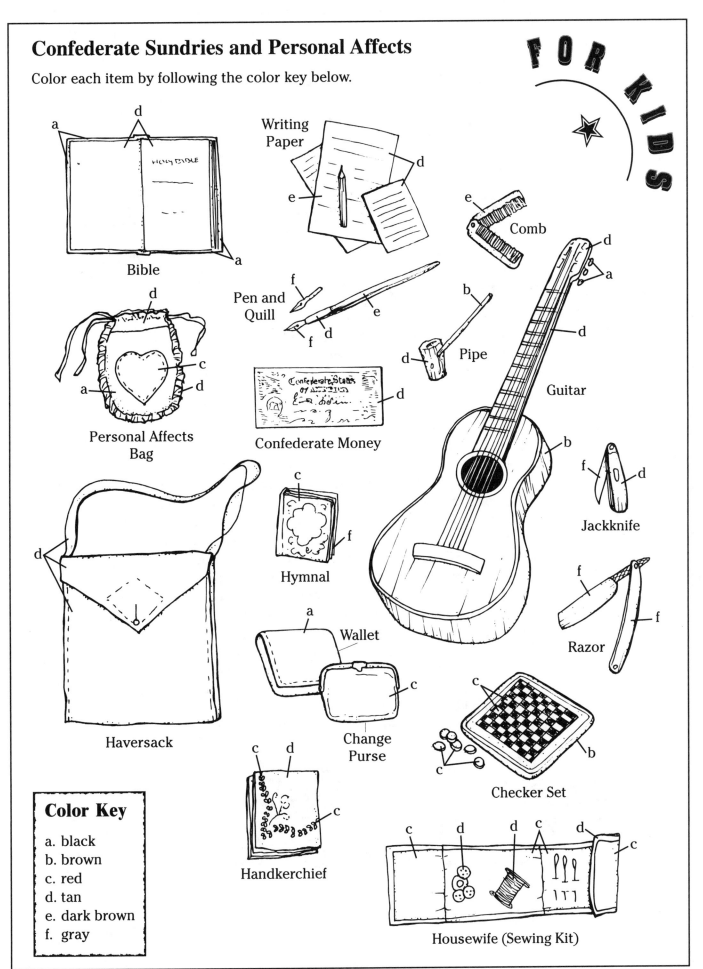

FOR KIDS

Bible

Writing Paper

Comb

Pen and Quill

Pipe

Guitar

Personal Affects Bag

Confederate Money

Jackknife

Razor

Haversack

Hymnal

Wallet

Change Purse

Checker Set

Handkerchief

Housewife (Sewing Kit)

Color Key

a. black
b. brown
c. red
d. tan
e. dark brown
f. gray

Inventions of War

BACKGROUND INFORMATION

Prior to the Civil War, foot soldiers fought with ancient muskets, sabers, and shotguns. Naval battles were fought in wooden ships. All this changed as inventions emerged that forever changed the way wars were fought.

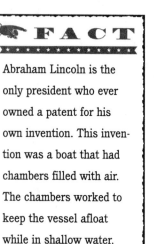
Airship

The Naval War

The South became the inventors of new forms of warfare for ships. But the lack of equipment, machinery, and metals limited their ability to be completely effective. One of their first inventions was an "ironclad" warship.

The ironclad came about shortly after Virginia seceded from the Union. The U.S. Navy had quickly evacuated their ships ported in the Norfolk, Virginia harbor. Rather than have their ships fall into rebel hands, the Union had them destroyed. One of these ships, the wooden steam frigate *USS Merrimack*, was only partially in ruin. Within a short period of time, the Confederates raised the sunken *Merrimack* from the shallow water. They rebuilt the wooden ship with armor plating, added casement ports for ten guns, and redesigned its hull to deter cannon fire. The Rebels then renamed their new ironclad, the *CSS Virginia*.

The Union Navy scrambled to create their own version of an ironclad warship that would stop the newly converted *Virginia*. Swedish-born inventor, John Ericsson, designed the North's first ironclad called the *USS Monitor*. This ship was protected by 4 1/2" (11.25 cm) of iron plating throughout the vessel. Nicknamed the "cheesebox on a raft," the *Monitor* was smaller and had fewer guns than the *Virginia*. Still, the *Monitor's* two guns had the unique capability of being able to revolve on a turret and fire in rotation. Both the *Virginia* and the *Monitor* were equally lethal.

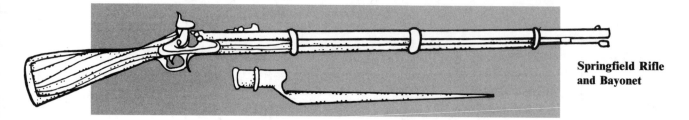
Springfield Rifle and Bayonet

On the 9th of March, both ships engaged in a furious sea battle that lasted for over four hours. The *Virginia* eventually withdrew because of its exhausted crew and because it was beginning to leak and have engine problems. Little damage was done to either ship. Nevertheless, this action signified a new era in sea warfare. Iron and steam would now replace wood and sails.

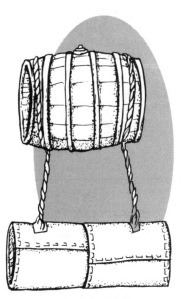

Hunley Submarine

The Confederates also pioneered other naval inventions. One was the "torpedo boat." This half-submerged vessel carried a long beam. A can or torpedo, filled with gunpowder was attached to the end of the beam. This apparatus was dragged through the water and exploded when it hit its target. Other inventions included underwater mines made from beer kegs and gunpowder, and gunboats converted from Mississippi ferryboats.

In 1863, the first working submarine—the *CSS HL Hunley*, named after its inventor—was in operation. It took several trials and the loss of many lives, including the inventor's, before the submarine proved seaworthy. The *Hunley* had no engine but was operated by an eight-man crew who cranked a propeller. Candles were the source of interior light for the men. Its crew was able to survive under the water for two and a half hours. The *Hunley* was also designed to tow a 200-foot (61-meter) rope with a bomb attached. As the submarine passed under an enemy warship, the bomb hit the ship and exploded. Unfortunately, sinking the Union warship also took the submarine and its hapless crew with it.

Pook turtles, or gunboats, were used in the Union river fleets. Named after their inventor, Samuel M. Pook, these ships were also plated with iron. The Pook turtles were powered by coal and propelled by a paddle wheel. The Pook turtles proved to be instrumental in the success of the Union's western campaigns.

Torpedo Made from Beer Keg

Gatling Gun

The Air War

Hot-air balloons were first employed by the North for intelligence-gathering of troop movements. Renown aeronautic scientist, Thaddeus Sobieski Lowe, became the chief of the first Federal Balloon

Corps. Through the course of the war, Lowe and his team built seven airships. The airships were made of silk and operated by hydrogen gas. The largest of these was the *Intrepid*. It was 32,000 cubic feet (906m³) in size and required 1,200 (1,097m) yards of silk.

Hand Grenade

The lack of materials did not hamper the Rebels' desire to build their own airship fleets. Their balloons were made from silk dresses provided by patriotic southern women.

The Land War

One of the most important inventions of the war was a refined bullet soldiers dubbed the "Minie Ball." Its creator, Claude Minié, developed this cylindrical bullet with a 1" slug. The newly designed slug enabled the bullet to spin out from the rifle's muzzle at great speed.

The Springfield rifle musket became the gun of choice for soldiers during the Civil War. This rifle had a better range and was more accurate than the ancient flint-lock or smoothbore muskets. However, it weighed up to ten pounds and was awkward to use. Also, preparing the gun to shoot a Minie Ball was time-consuming. A soldier poured gunpowder into the rifle barrel. Then, he pulled a paper-wrapped Minie Ball out from it's pouch, ripping the paper off with his teeth. The ball was dropped into the muzzle and thrust into the barrel with a ramrod. The soldier then attached a "percussion" cap to the musket hammer. Finally, the soldier cocked the hammer, aimed the gun, and fired. The average soldier could load his rifle ten times in five minutes.

The "coffee-mill" gun, as President Lincoln called it, marked the beginning of the machine gun era. These guns were designed in such a way that bullets dropped from a hopper into a revolving cylinder. A soldier would turn a crank that rapidly released the bullets. A later model had six-barreled guns encased in a steel jacket. Named after its inventor, Dr. Richard Gatling, the Gatling gun became the first machine gun to be adopted by any army.

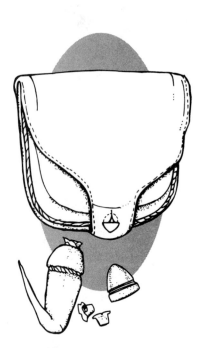

Minie Ball, Percussion Caps, and Paper Cartridge

☞ **F A C T**
★★★★★★★★★★★★★★
Thaddeaus Sobieski Lowe and his airship crew made over 3,000 flights into Confederate territory.

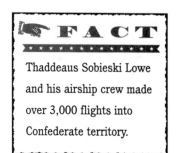

Artillery Mortar

The Sweat Box

President Lincoln proudly toured his fleet of naval battleships. While on a small steamer boat, he noticed a narrow door with long sturdy iron locks. "What is this?" the president asked. "This is a sweat box," replied the captain of the steamer. "We use this box to punish insubordinate seamen. A man sits in it and is subjected to steam and heat. Rarely does a man commit the same offense again."

President Lincoln knew that thousands of navy men were punished this way. So, he insisted that he give it a try. He took off his black stovepipe hat and awkwardly positioned himself inside. The sweat box could not have been any more than 3 feet (.9 m) in length and width. "When I rap on the door, let me out," the president demanded.

The sweat box door was closed and President Lincoln sat alone in the dark. Suffocatingly hot steam pushed through the pipes. It wasn't more than three minutes when the men heard the president's quick raps.

The sweat box door was quickly opened. "That was a wretched experience," President Lincoln said flatly. "It is time for me to decide that this type of punishment is not only unnecessary but also inhumane. No such enclosure as this sweat box will ever be allowed on a ship flying the American flag," Lincoln insisted.

Every sailor in the Union Navy heard this story and all were grateful to President Lincoln. The European navies of Great Britain, France, and Germany heard the same story and immediately followed action. Never again was a sweat box allowed on any vessel flying under the flag of a civilized nation.

GROUP PROJECT

Hunley Submarine Whirligig Garden

Whirligigs were popular wind toys before and during the Civil War era. Although similar to weather vane, whirligigs had no real purpose. People often placed them in their gardens, on fences, or in front of their barns.

Materials

- balsa wood panel, 1/4" x 4" x 24" (.5 cm x 10 cm x 60 cm)
- wooden dowel, 3/8" x 36" (1 cm x .9 m)
- X-acto® knife
- hand saw
- white acrylic primer
- sharp pencil
- tape

- black permanent marker
- hammer
- carbon paper
- white glue
- nail
- acrylic paints
- 19th-century Crafters Vinegar Paint as described below (optional)

Optional Materials for the balsa wood: Heavy cardboard for the base panel and empty paper-towel rolls in place of the dowel. These materials will not stand up to weather elements as well as the wood.

Crafter's Vinegar Paint

- powdered poster or tempera paints
- 1/4 cup (63 mL) distilled vinegar
- dishwashing detergent
- 1/2 teaspoon (2.5 mL) sugar
- mixing bowls for each color of vinegar paint
- paintbrushes for details
- clear varnish

Making the Paint

You will make each of your colors with the same formula. Mix the vinegar, sugar, and three to four drops of liquid detergent together until the sugar slowly dissolves. Add 2 tablespoons (30 mL) of one paint color to the vinegar solution and mix. The mixture dries quickly once it is applied.

Making a Balsa Whirligig

Follow the same process for cardboard whirligigs.

1. Paint the balsa wood panel on both sides with the white primer. Let dry.

2. Copy the submarine design on page 47. Tape it down to the balsa wood panel.

3. Slip carbon paper underneath the design and follow the lines with a sharp pencil. Make sure to press down hard enough so that the carbon paper marks the wood. (Figure 1)

4. Using the X-acto® knife, cut out the submarine design on the wood by following the outside lines made from the carbon paper. (Figure 2)

Figure 1

5. Paint the submarine design on both sides. Outline in black permanent marker. Let dry. Also, paint the dowel white. Set aside.

6. Make the submarine propeller by cutting two additional pieces of wood from the scraps of balsa. Follow the submarine instructions.

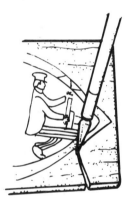

7. Cross the propeller pieces and glue their middles together. (Figure 3)

8. After the glue has dried on the propeller, hammer a nail through its center. Move the nail around to make the hole wide enough for the wood to spin around. (Figure 4)

Figure 2

9. Nail the propeller to the tail end of the submarine. (Figure 5)

10. The dowel is used as the whirligig's standing support. Score the tip of the dowel with a hand saw from it's middle and down 1/2" (1.25 cm). Press and glue the middle of the submarine into the slit. (Figure 6)

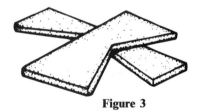

Figure 3

11. When the whirligig is dry, place it outside by sticking the bottom of the dowel into the ground.

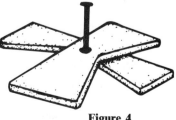

Figure 4

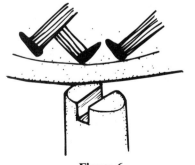

Figure 6

Figure 5

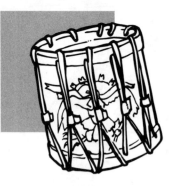

INDIVIDUAL PROJECT

Mini Drums

Soldiers learned to follow the beat of drums and march in unison. The drum beats were a form of communicating instructions when the men could not hear their commander's orders during battle.

Confederate

Union

Materials

- 20 empty one-gallon ice-cream containers (found at ice-cream stores)
- chamois (found at hardware stores) or drum head (found at music stores)
- S-hooks
- transfer paper
- tape
- black permanent marker
- lacing
- hole punch
- spray paint (white or blue)
- enamel paints (colors to match are red, yellow, white, blue, and brown)
- small paintbrushes
- electrical tape
- pencil
- scissors

Figure 1

Figure 2

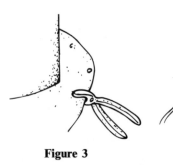

Figure 3

Figure 4

1. Paint the outside of the ice-cream container white (Confederate) or blue (Union), and let dry.

2. Enlarge Union or Confederate emblems at the top of this page to fit one side of the container.

3. Copy the design by taping down the transfer paper (sticky side down) to the container. Place the design on top. Copy the design by following the lines with a pencil. (Figure 1)

4. Paint with desired colors and outline in black. Let dry. Enamels are long-lasting but require more time to dry.

5. Set the container onto the chamois. Cut around it, leaving 2" (5 cm) all the way around. (Figure 2)

6. Punch evenly-spaced holes with a hole punch, approximately 3" (7.5 cm) apart and at least 1/2" (1.25 cm) from the edge. (Figure 3)

7. Knot one end of the lacing and pull through to the first hole of the chamois. Pull the lacing down and hook to the bottom of the container with an S-hook, then repeat. (Figure 4)

8. Once you've completed the lacing, tie it secure. Then, take the electrical tape and tape two laces together at a time. Repeat the process.

The Hunley Submarine

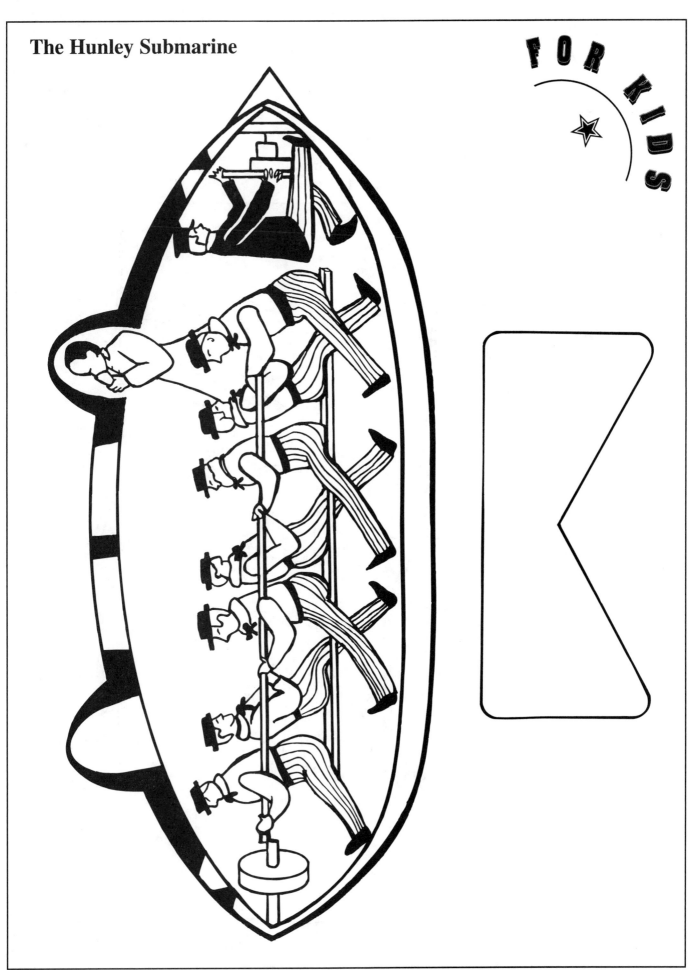

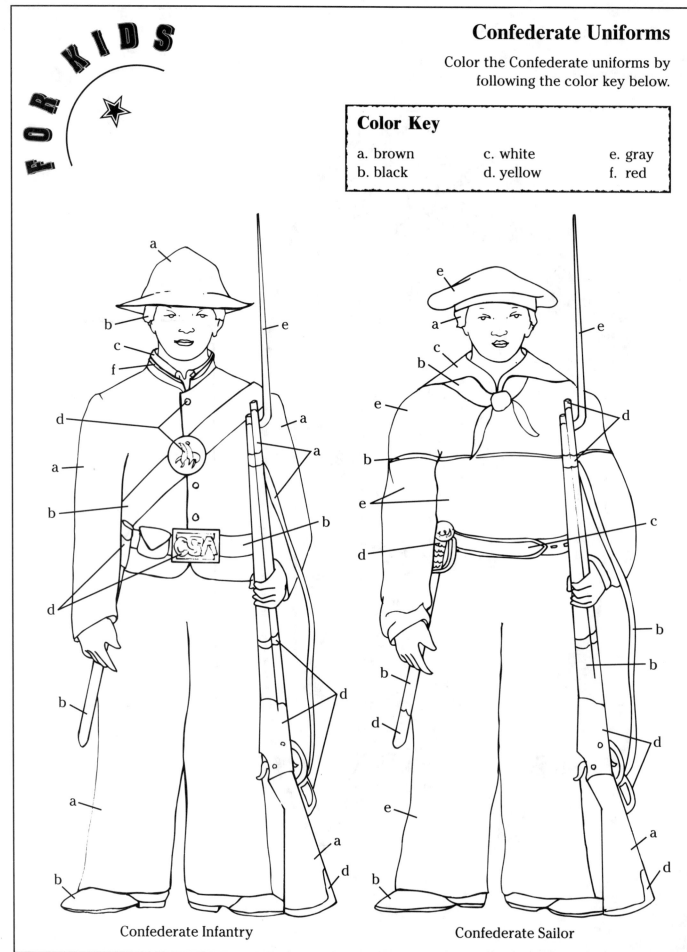

Confederate Uniforms

Color the Confederate uniforms by following the color key below.

Color Key

a. brown   c. white   e. gray
b. black   d. yellow   f. red

Confederate Infantry

Confederate Sailor

Teacher's Note: Use this page as a flat coloring sheet.
© Good Apple GA13010

Confederate Naval Artifacts and Accouterments

Color the Confederate artifacts and accouterments by following the color key below.

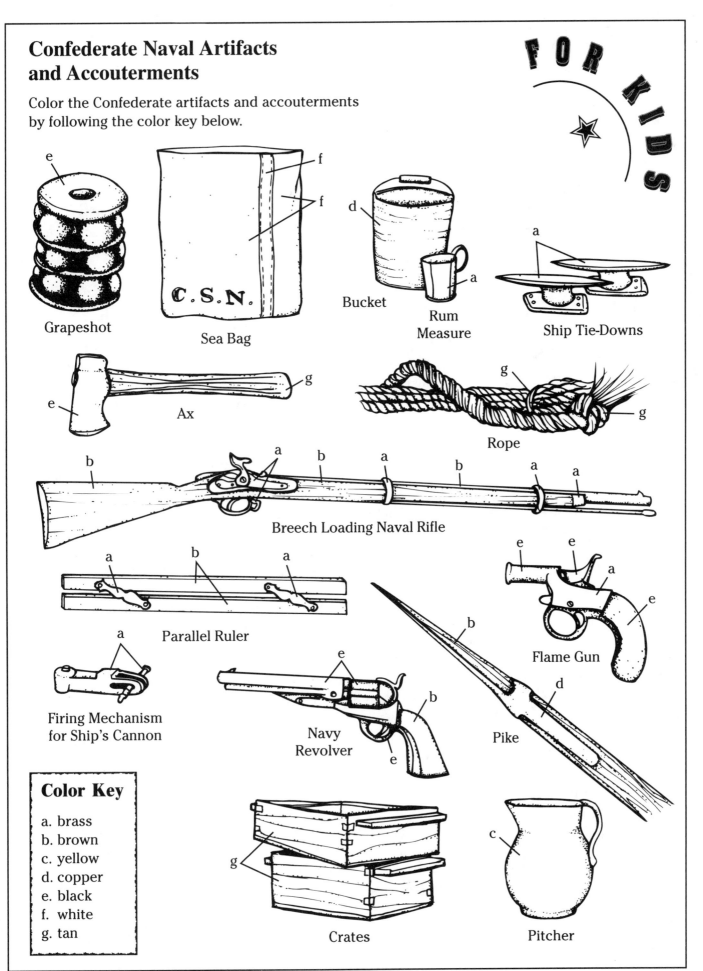

Grapeshot

Sea Bag

Bucket

Rum Measure

Ship Tie-Downs

Ax

Rope

Breech Loading Naval Rifle

Parallel Ruler

Flame Gun

Firing Mechanism for Ship's Cannon

Navy Revolver

Pike

Color Key

a. brass
b. brown
c. yellow
d. copper
e. black
f. white
g. tan

Crates

Pitcher

The Secret War

BACKGROUND INFORMATION

While the armies of the North and South clashed against each other, spies from both sides fought their own battles in clandestine adventures. They wore disguises, hopped trains, and hid in swamps. Their secret messages were hidden in hair, jewelry, dolls, and even emptied eggshells. Many lost their reputations and even their lives. Still, their courage and innovations added a twist to the American Civil War.

Spy Brigades

The first government intelligence agency began just before Lincoln's inauguration. The agency was headed by an immigrant from Scotland, Allan Pinkerton. In 1850, Pinkerton started one of the country's first detective agencies. Railroad security was his specialty. When he was hired by the federal government, his duties broadened into intelligence gathering and espionage activities.

Under Pinkerton's direction, brave and cunning agents penetrated the Confederate forces. One of the most valuable Federal agents was Timothy Webster. His risky missions often took him deep into the heart of the South. Webster had the ability to gain the trust of many Confederate officers who unknowingly passed vital information to this Federal spy. Webster's life was constantly in jeopardy. He survived by his wits as he leaped from trains, endured shipwrecks, and escaped counter-spy attacks. Eventually he was captured and hanged as a traitor. Another Federal agent was John Scobell, a former slave. Scobell moved through the rebel lines as a vendor. He picked up bits of information by eavesdropping on Rebel officers. When in danger of being exposed, Scobell purposefully stammered and threw epileptic fits. Confederate officers believed that Scobell could never operate as a spy.

Pinkerton had his hands full with Rebel spies living in Washington, D.C. One of the most notorious of these was the Washington socialite, Rose O'Neal Greenhow. An attractive widow, Greenhow used her charms on senators and federal officers who had access to classified information. Greenhow passed this important information through the lines by having her female agents carry cryptic notes tucked into their hair.

At the helm of the Confederate secret service was Captain William Norris. Norris wanted to penetrate the Federal War Department. He enlisted the aid of many southern sympathizers in clandestine meetings held in churches, alleys, and even on the steps of federal buildings.

**Doll with Hollow Head—
Used to Smuggle Medicine
Across the Lines.**

FACT

The first Tennessee Cavalry worked as scouts and spies for the Federal Army. Because of their efforts, a network of informants, particularly women, were able to pass vital information through enemy lines to the Union authorities.

50

Army Scouts and Ordinary Citizens

Generals on the front lines relied on their own scouts for information. One in particular was Major General Ulysses S. Grant. After being caught with inadequate information on a Confederate surprise attack at Shiloh, Tennessee, Grant sought to create his own espionage ring. Spymaster for Grant's legendary operation was Brigadier General Grenville M. Dodge. Grenville and Grant developed a network of 117 agents made up of soldiers, double agents, and ordinary citizens. The agents were identified by numbers so their names would be protected.

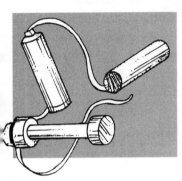

Torpedo Used for Blowing Up Bridges

One agent who proved to be instrumental to General Grant's success later in the war was southern-born Elizabeth Van Lew. Even before the war, Van Lew was known as "Crazy Bet." This was partly because she was a southern abolitionist who set all of her slaves free long before the war. She even sent some of her slaves to be educated in the North. During the course of the war, "Crazy Bet" magnified her oddity by walking the Richmond streets while mumbling to herself. She wore unkept clothes and messed her hair to enhance the illusion. In her "crazy" disguise, Van Lew entered the nearby Libby prison which held Union soldiers. She carried baskets of books, food, and medicine for prisoners.

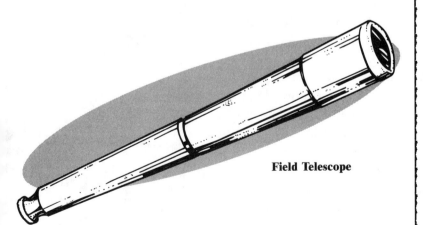

Field Telescope

FACT

Some well-known spies:

BELLE BOYD—She began her career as a respected spy and courier for the Confederate Army in the Shenandoah Valley at the age of 17. She risked her life to bring detailed reports of the Union Army movements to Stonewall Jackson's headquarters, but was finally captured toward the end of the war. Her captor, Union Navy Lieutenant Samuel Hardinge, ended up marrying her and left the U.S. Navy to join the Confederate service. After the war, Belle turned to lecturing and writing her memoirs. She appeared in American and British theaters until the 1900s.

MISS S. EMMA E. EDMONDS—She worked as a Canadian nurse and often disguised herself as a black man. In her disguise, she was able to cross Confederate lines and bring back vital information to the Union Army.

CHARLES HEIDSICK—He disguised himself as a bartender and worked on several Mississippi steamers. While on the ships, he overheard a great deal of information which he passed to the Rebels.

DR. WILLIAM T. PASSMORE—He dressed in rags and pretended to be a half-wit. He wandered through Union camps selling produce from a cart. The information he gathered went directly to the Rebel Army.

PAULINE CUSHMAN—A well-known actress, the southern-born Cushman served as a spy for the Union Army. When she was finally captured and scheduled to be executed, Union soldiers liberated the town she was held in and rescued her. Cushman returned to her work as an actress following the war, and like Boyd, regaled her audiences with tales of her exploits as a secret agent of the Union.

While in the prison, Van Lew overheard the idle chatter of prison guards and even pried information from the prison's commandant. Van Lew also created a secret written code in which she and the prisoners communicated. She read the hidden messages that were lightly underlined in the books she loaned to the men. Then, she deciphered the information and hid the messages in emptied eggshells and produce baskets. Her agents carried the baskets with the hidden messages through the lines until they safely reached General Grant. As time wore on, Van Lew's spying techniques grew more sophisticated. With one of her ex-slaves, she was able to penetrate the home of Confederate President Jefferson Davis and gain valuable information. At the end of the war, Van Lew had seven courier stations and five relay stations in place. Her system of retrieving and sending information to the proper authorities was so fast that the flowers she sent along with the decoded messages were still fresh when they reached their destination.

Spying Techniques and Advancements

In 1861, telegraphs were a primary source of communication. Both sides continually broke through the telegraph lines to hear the dots and dashes of secrets being transmitted. Because of this, new communication systems were quickly put in place. New systems came in the form of flag signals, telegraph ciphers, and decoding devices.

At the beginning of the war, the Union Army constructed four signal towers. Men stood on the signal tower platform and systematically moved the flags to produce a specific code. Miles away, another person would peer through their field glasses and decipher the flag codes. The deciphered information would be passed to the commanders in charge. However, Yankees and Rebels used the same codes. Anyone who had a telescope and knowledge of the codes could intercept the hidden message. Confederate Chief Spymaster Captain William Norris, devised his own signals by using colored balls that were arranged up and down the signal flagpoles. This device allowed his signal corps to send secret messages. As time went on, the secret codes for both the flags and telegraphs were cracked by the enemy. It became necessary to constantly develop new means of sending messages. Both Federals and Confederates alike developed their own cipher disks. These disks were used in recognizing the random sequence of letters that held secret meaning.

Signal Tower

Signal Flags

LEGEND

Pauline Cushman Borrows a Young Man's Suit

Miss Pauline Cushman stayed at a hotel in a small southern town. She had her heart set on gathering Rebel secrets, but she needed a way to conceal herself. In the hotel was a teenage boy who was close to her height and weight. So, she devised a plan to steal his clothes.

When all were asleep, Pauline crept into the boy's room. The suit was laid over a chair. She grabbed it and slipped out of the room. Once dressed in the boy's clothes, Pauline borrowed a fast horse she found in the stables.

Pauline galloped through the woods until she came upon a Rebel camp. Pauline hid behind a thick group of trees and intently listened to their quiet conversations. Unfortunately, she accidentally stepped on a dry stick. The startled men jumped to their feet, mounted their horses, and chased Pauline through the woods.

Pauline was an expert horsewoman and, for a short time, she lost her pursuers. But she still needed a way out. Finally, Pauline saw a wounded Yankee scout laying on the side of the road. She pleaded with the man to help her for they both knew he would soon die from his wounds. The scout agreed and she devised a plan.

Pauline fired her pistol into the air and the Rebels followed its sound. To their surprise, they found the boy they had been chasing standing over a Yankee soldier. Pauline shouted in her deepest voice, "I shot this Yankee and I'm just sorry there weren't others." The confused Rebels asked who she was. "I'm a farmer's son," she continued. The Rebel soldiers and Pauline lifted the wounded Yankee onto a horse and made their way back. When they passed an area with overgrown trees, Pauline slipped away. She hid her horse behind a rock and shot wildly into the air. The Rebels believed it was the Yankees and sped away.

Pauline found her way back to the hotel just before the sun rose. She brought the borrowed horse back to its stall, returned the suit to its sleeping owner, and went to sleep.

GROUP PROJECT

Codes and Ciphers

Secret codes became important tools for the spies and armies during the Civil War. This was particularly evident when telegraphs and signal flag codes were easy targets for the enemy who listened and watched. When the telegraph wires hummed the dots and dashes of letters, the translator would translate the code into letters. From the letters was coded information that needed to be deciphered. The Confederates used a cipher that was originally created by the Europeans over 400 years ago. A real code sent by Confederate President Jefferson Davis to General Kirby Smith looked like this "...HCDL-VWXMWIQIG KM..."

With this project, your students will learn to make the "diplomatic" cipher used by the Confederate Army. They will also learn how to send secret messages and "crack" each other's codes.

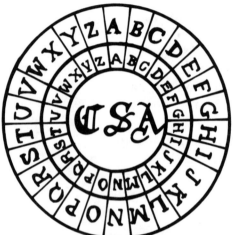

Materials

– two paper plates
– hole punch
– scissors
– black permanent marker
– brass-colored spray paint
– spray glue
– brass paper fastener

Before You Begin

Divide the class into teams. Have each team secretly discuss which "key" letter they will use to decipher and write codes.

Making the Cipher

1. Each student should have their own cipher. Copy the ciphers on page 57. Cut out the ciphers. Spray the back of each cipher with glue and secure it onto a paper plate. (Figure 1)

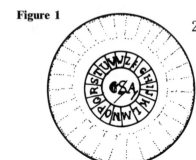

Figure 1

2. Lightly spray both ciphers with brass-colored paint and let dry. Do not saturate. Redraw any letters covered with the brass spray paint using the permanent marker.

3. Punch a hole in the middle of both plates. Set the small disk on top of the large disk and press the brass fastener through. (Figure 2)

54

Practice the Cipher Using a Key Letter

4. Write the word Rebel on a sheet of paper.

5. Letter *C* will be your key letter for this practice run. Move the small disk letter *C* to the large disk, letter *A*. (Figure 3)

6. Do not move the disk. Note the letter *R* on the small disk. Above it on the large disk would be the letter *P*. Write *P* underneath.

7. The next letter is *E*. Find it on the small sphere. Above it on the large sphere is the letter *C*.

8. Follow this process until you have spelled out the entire word *Rebel* with the coded letters. These coded letters should look like: *PCDEJ*, if letter *C* was the key.

Writing Your Own Secret Messages in Groups

9. Have each group member write his or her own secret message in code using a key letter. Keep the message simple at first, related, in some way, to the Civil War. More sophisticated messages can be developed later.

10. Have group members trade messages with each other. They will then try to decipher the codes using the cipher disk.

11. Have students trade the codes with students in other groups.

12. Decode the messages by randomly selecting different letters in order to "crack" the code. Time the students. Whoever "cracks" the first enemy code is the classroom Spy Master.

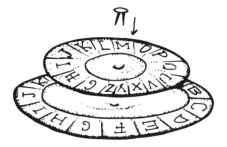

Figure 2

Figure 3

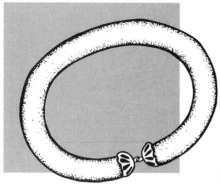

INDIVIDUAL PROJECT

Spy Bracelet

One way secret messages were passed over the lines was in women's jewelry. Inside the jewelry were hollowed-out secret compartments. Elizabeth Van Lew hid her secret cipher codes and messages in the back of her wristwatch, while others used their bracelets.

Figure 1

Figure 2

Materials

– jewelry end caps, 8 mm x 16 mm (found in craft stores)
– two 14 mm end bead caps
– two 2" (5 cm) gold eye pins
– epoxy glue or jewelry craft glue
– vinyl fuel hose, 3/8" x 8" (1 cm x 20 cm) (found in hardware stores)
– gold enamel spray
– India ink (optional)
– crow-quill pen and nib (optional)
– onion paper, 2" x 1/2" (5 cm x 1.25 cm) (optional)

---

1. Cut the vinyl hose to loosely fit around the student's wrist. Paint the vinyl hose gold and let dry.

2. Stick the gold pin into the jewelry end cap and crimp. (Figure 1)

3. Glue crimped end cap to the vinyl hose and let dry. (Figure 2)

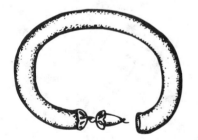

Figure 3

4. Secure another end cap and end bead cap together with a pin. Make sure the bead cap's nose points out. Crimp all hardware together. (Figure 3)

5. Lightly press the end bead cap into the vinyl hose. This will act as a stopper as well a clip that will hold the bracelet's shape. Do not shove or force the bead cap inside the vinyl hose as it may become difficult to pull open. (Figure 4)

6. Write a secret code on a small piece of onion paper using the cipher instructions on pages 54 and 55. For a more authentic project, use the crow quill pen and India ink.

7. Fold the message, slip it into the secret compartment in the bracelet, and pass it on to be decoded. (Figure 5)

Figure 4

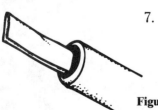

Figure 5

56

Confederate Cipher

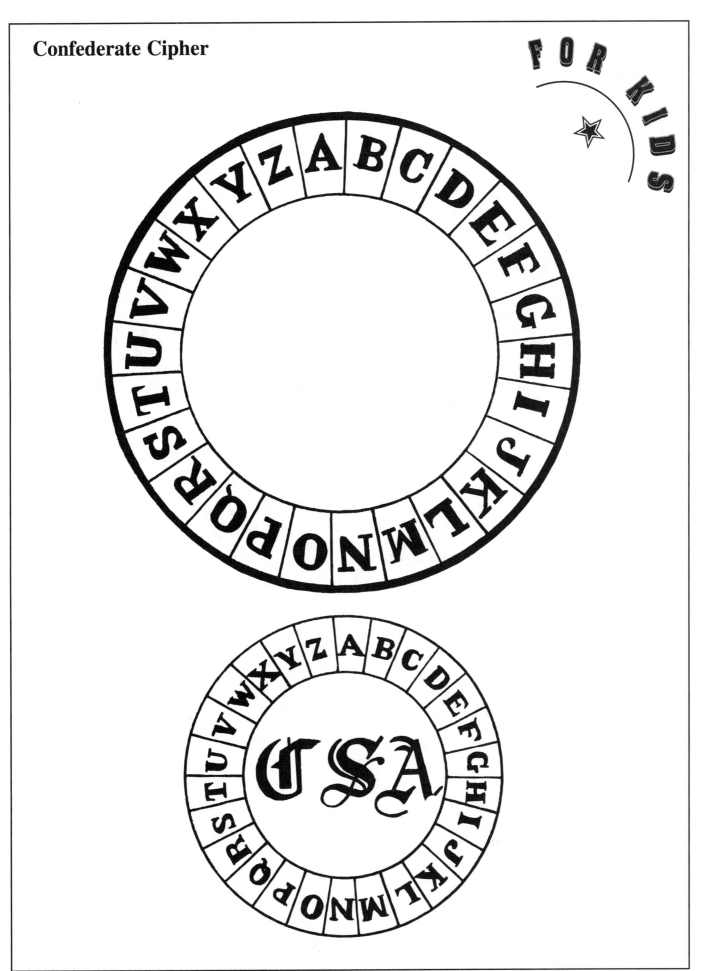

Teacher's Note: Use this page as a flat coloring sheet or enlarge each item to use in one of the special projects described on pages 54 and 55.
© Good Apple GA13010

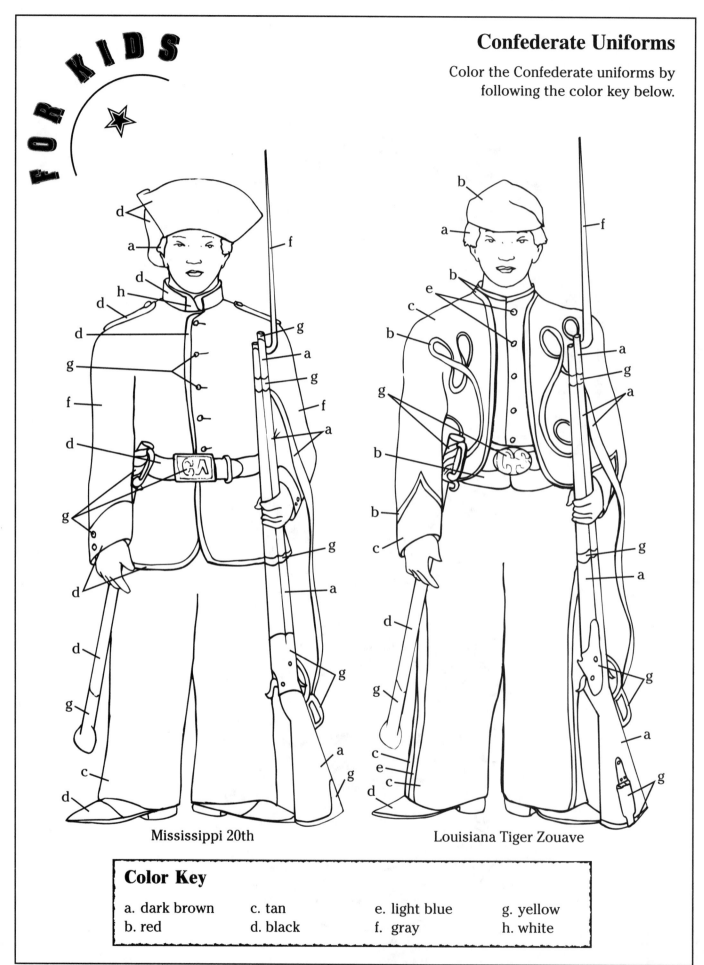

Confederate Uniforms

Color the Confederate uniforms by following the color key below.

Mississippi 20th

Louisiana Tiger Zouave

Color Key

a. dark brown	c. tan	e. light blue	g. yellow
b. red	d. black	f. gray	h. white

Confederate Army Camp Artifacts

Color the Confederate camp artifacts
by following the color key below.

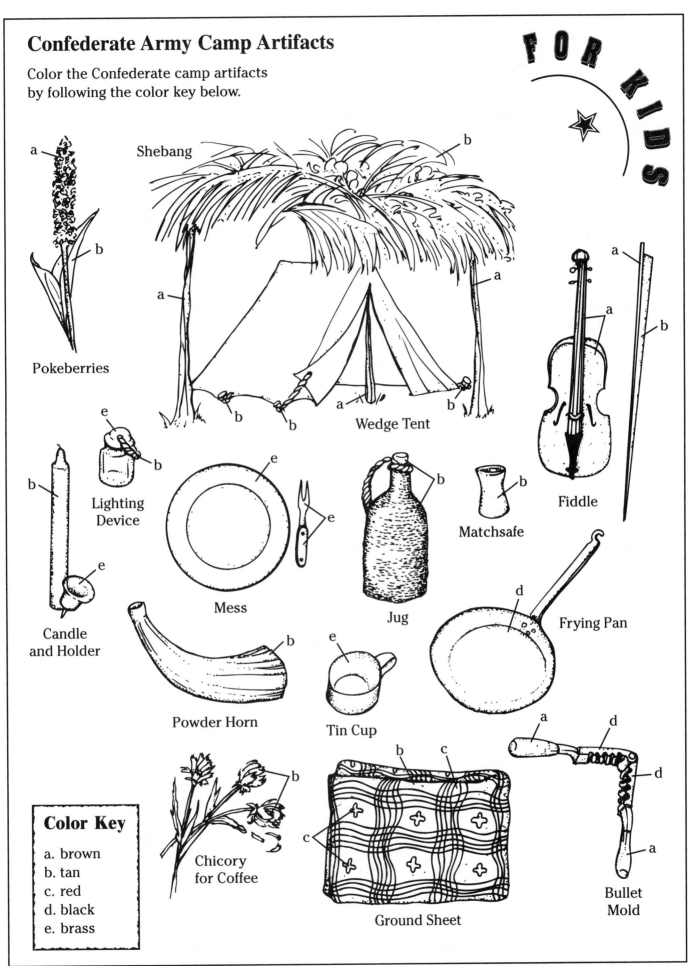

a

Pokeberries

b

Shebang

b

a

a

Wedge Tent

b

b

a

b

Fiddle

a

a

e

b

Lighting
Device

b

Candle
and Holder

e

e

Mess

e

e

Powder Horn

b

Tin Cup

e

b

Jug

b

Matchsafe

d

Frying Pan

a

d

d

a

Bullet
Mold

Color Key

a. brown
b. tan
c. red
d. black
e. brass

Chicory
for Coffee

b

Ground Sheet

b c

c

The Progressing War

BACKGROUND INFORMATION

The Union Army was larger and better equipped than the Rebel Army, but it lacked strong leadership. It took President Lincoln nearly four years before he found a leader who could successfully steer the entire Union Army and end the war. As for the South, generals such as Robert E. Lee, "Stonewall" Jackson, Joseph Johnston, Jubal Early, and Nathan Bedford Forrest made the best of their limited resources. They were able to rally support from their men and continually led them victoriously into battle.

Field Carriage with Cannon

Generals of the Peninsula Campaign

After the first battle at Manassas, General McClellan kept his Union Army immobilized. Believing that the Rebel forces were stronger, he continued to collect more men and supplies. After a lengthy delay, President Lincoln grew frustrated with him and demanded that he move the Union Army to take Richmond, Virginia. Instead of a direct attack, McClellan shifted soldiers down and around the Virginia coast to come up from behind. This approach gave the Rebels ample time to fortify their stronghold and successfully prepare for battle.

At this time, the northern armies faced many disasters on the Virginia battlefield because McClellan lacked aggressiveness in his war strategy. President Lincoln dismissed him and placed General John Pope in charge of the "new" Army of Virginia. This army consisted of Union forces in the Shenandoah Valley plus elements of McClellan's Army of the Potomac. Pope was known as an aggressive leader. However, under his direction, the Union Army failed to win major battles. This was particularly evident during the Second Battle of Bull Run, where they were severely defeated despite outnumbering the Rebels two to one. President Lincoln relieved Pope from duty and sent him to Minnesota to fight the Sioux. Lincoln replaced Pope with McClellan again.

By September 1862, Lee led his 50,000 Rebel soldiers across the Potomac to invade the North in order to seize the fertile land of Maryland. Once again, McClellan was hesitant to move until two of his sergeants found a small package that contained three cigars and a copy of General Lee's orders. The orders spelled out the entire Rebel campaign in Maryland. McClellan finally felt confident that his massive army would successfully meet the Rebels on the battlefield.

On September 17, 1862, the Battle of Antietam began. McClellan's Army of the Potomac clashed with Lee's Rebel Army of North Virginia. It was the single bloodiest one-day battle of the war. By nightfall, Lee made up his mind that his Rebels would retreat. McClellan, already in a strong position, again slowed his troops from advancing toward the Rebels. His lack of action gave Lee the opportunity to slip away back to southern territory. President Lincoln was furious and fired McClellan once and for all. The president's replacement was General Ambrose Burnside. But, within a few months, Burnside nearly shattered his army at Fredericksburg

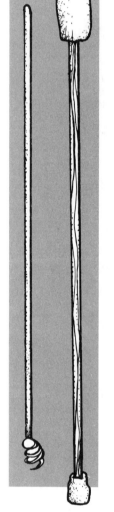

Field Gun Items

Shebang

because of fruitless charges against entrenched Confederates. President Lincoln immediately replaced General Burnside with Major General Joseph Hooker. Hooker was an ambitious general and his men loved him. But just as the others, Hooker also lost his nerve when it came to fighting the Rebel forces. This was particularly evident in a critical battle at Chancellorsville in May 1863. During this battle, Hooker and his well-equipped troops were soundly defeated. Because of the constant blundering and near misses on the battlefield, President Lincoln was forced to replace General Hooker with General George Meade.

Bugle

The Western Campaign and the Army of the Tennessee

The Tennessee, Cumberland, and Mississippi Rivers were major arteries of travel and trade for the Confederacy. The Union Army of the Tennessee and the U.S. Navy worked together to secure these vital areas. Gunboats were used to attack the Rebel forts on the rivers, army troops fought the land battles, and the navy blockaded the southern ports off the Gulf of Mexico. Within the first six months of 1862, the Union Army controlled most of Missouri and Tennessee.

One of the most devastating land battles up to this time was a battle in Shiloh, Tennessee, which took place in April. Under the direction of Ulysses S. Grant, the Union won the battle despite an initial Confederate surprise attack, but the losses were great. In many respects, this battle served to open a gateway for Union troops to later occupy the major southern cities of Cornith, Memphis, and Nashville.

By 1863, there were only two vital ports left in Confederate hands, Port Hudson in Louisiana and Port Vicksburg in Mississippi. On July 4, 1863, Grant and his Army of the Tennessee seized Vicksburg, with Port Hudson falling days later. The Union was finally in control of the Mississippi River and was able to cut Louisiana, Arkansas, and Texas off from the rest of the Confederacy.

F A C T

General Meade had received orders from President Lincoln to replace General Hooker on June 28, 1863. The next day, with little time to prepare, Meade commanded his Army of the Potomac to advance toward Gettysburg to contest Lee's forces, which were approaching that sleepy Pennsylvania town.

The Changing Tide

By 1863, the success of the Army of North Virginia prompted General Lee to march north once more and take Harrisburg, the capital of Pennsylvania. He believed that a serious defeat on Union soil would pressure the federal government to seek peace.

On June 30th, a Rebel brigade under Rebel General Henry Heth, was sent to Gettysburg to obtain supplies—particularly shoes. In the early morning hours of July 1, these Rebels accidentally came upon the Union cavalry, and the Battle of Gettysburg began. Both groups were startled and unprepared, but with fierce fighting, the Rebels pushed the Yankees back. By the second day, the Yankees found a defense position on top of a ridge known as Cemetery Ridge. On the third day, Rebel troops, under General George Pickett, charged up this ridge. Within one hour, 12,000 men were gunned down. On July 4th, General Lee ordered his army to retreat. He was so horrified at the slaughter, that he apologized to his men. He later offered to resign his post.

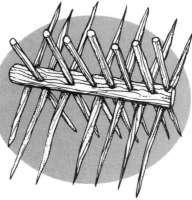

Chevaux-de-frise

LEGEND

Gettysburg Address

President Lincoln was invited to make a few remarks at the dedication of the Gettysburg War Cemetery, but the day before the festivities, he became ill. A towel was placed on his head and he closed his eyes. Tucked away in his pocket was a rough copy of his speech. The president felt uneasy, especially since he was scheduled to speak after the gifted orator, Edward Everett. Lincoln had always admired Everett's ability to capture an audience's attention with his long, dramatic speeches and deep resonate voice. Furthermore, he knew that public opinion of him was waning because the war was still raging without an end in sight.

On the morning of November 19, 1863, Lincoln arrived at the unfinished cemetery. Edward Everett spoke for over two hours and kept the audience spellbound. They enthusiastically applauded when he finished. Then, it was Lincoln's turn. He stood up at the podium, looked over the audience, and spoke in his squeaky voice.

"Four score and seven years ago, our fathers brought forth on this continent, a new nation, conceived in liberty, and dedicated to the proposition that all men are created equal." He glanced down at his notes, then went straight to the purpose of why the audience was there—the dedication of the Gettysburg Cemetery.

"The brave men, living and dead, who struggled here, have consecrated it far above our poor power to add or detract. The world will little not, nor long remember, what we say here, but it can never forget what they did here." Then he concluded… "and that this nation, under God, shall have a new birth of freedom; and that this government of the people, by the people, and for the people, shall not perish from the earth." The audience was stunned and few clapped. Most were unaware that the speech had begun and ended. Lincoln was sure that his speech was a disaster.

The Gettysburg Address, no longer than ten lines, took less than three minutes to deliver. Still, it has earned prominence as one of our nation's most famous speeches. All the while, it was rehearsed, written, and delivered by a man who suffered from a mild case of smallpox.

62

GROUP PROJECT

Gettysburg Address
Paper-Making Memorial

The Gettysburg Address is perhaps one of the nation's most important speeches to date. There are five autographed copies of this speech that President Lincoln wrote out himself. The first two copies were given to his secretaries, John Hay and John Nicolay. The copy given to Nicolay is exhibited at the Library of Congress and is considered to be the earliest draft. Experts believe this because the first page is written in pen on the executive mansion stationary, while the second copy is written in pencil on lined paper. Based on eyewitness accounts, Lincoln pulled this speech out from his pocket before he delivered it. The folds and creases in the Nicolay version also lead the experts to believe that this is the original copy.

The other three copies were written for charitable reasons. Speaker Edward Everett, who was at Gettysburg and delivered his two-hour speech before Lincoln, also received a copy. This copy is now in the Illinois State Historical Library. The Bliss copy was made for Colonel Bliss and is now on display in the Lincoln Room of the White House. The final copy of the Gettysburg Address was made for historian George Bancroft and is held at Cornell University.

Before You Begin

Have students read the Gettysburg Address on page 62. Then, ask students why they feel that this is was an important speech during the Civil War, and why they feel it is so important today. Then, explain any difficult words or concepts so that the speech might become more meaningful to them.

Materials

- foam plates or meat trays
- rubber cement
- X-acto® knife
- tape
- cotton linter
- white or manila recycled paper—ripped in small postage stamp pieces
- blender
- oblong washtub (big enough to hold your mold frames)
- water to fill tub
- sharp pen or pencil

- strainer
- butter knife
- cold-water starch
- two 11" x 14" (27.5 cm x 35 cm) wooden frames
- fine netting, tulle, or window screen, 14" x 16" (35 cm x 40 cm)
- tacks
- absorbent cotton cloths
- pencil with eraser or cotton swabs
- crow-quill pen and nib
- India ink

Optional: For excellent paper-making, also purchase two 7" x 9" (17.5 cm x 22.5 cm) sheets of cotton linter found in craft stores. Rip it up and soak it along with your paper pulp.

Making the Presidential Seal

1. Enlarge the federal seal on page 67 to 2" or 3" (5 cm or 7.5 cm).

2. Glue two foam plates together with the rubber cement. Lay the design on top of the foam plates and tape down. Take a sharp pencil or pen and press into the design while following the lines. Make sure you leave a clear impression on the foam plate. (Figure 1)

3. Cut all the way through the foam plates with an X-acto® knife. Remember, the back of the seal is just as important for this project as the front, so cut it carefully. Set the seal aside until later in the paper-making stage. (Figure 2)

Making the Mold and Paper

4. Stretch the netting over one of the frames and tack down. Make sure that it is pulled tight. The other frame will remain the same. It will be the deckle and, later, it will help to form your paper. (Figure 3)

5. Make the paper by soaking it in water for over an hour so it softens. Add the cotton linter as well. Pour the strained paper into a blender and fill it 2/3 full of water. Blend paper until it becomes smooth and pulpy. Make sure the mixture remains watery, and continue the process.

6. Toss the mixture into the tub. Continue to make more pulp until you've made enough to sufficiently cover one frame.

7. Stir in 2 to 4 tablespoons (30 mL to 60 mL) of the cold starch into the pulp and stir well.

8. While the pulp is still floating, slip the mold and the deckle into the water at an angle. Make sure the mold is the bottom frame. (Figure 4)

9. Lay the mold and deckle (frames) in the water. They need to be in a flat position so that they will collect the pulp.

10. Pull the deckle and mold straight out of the water. Shake it off as if you were straining it and spread some of the fibers around. (Figure 5)

Figure 1

Figure 2

Figure 3

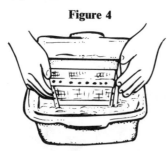

Figure 4

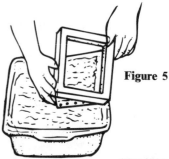

Figure 5

64

11. Pull the deckle off carefully and make sure the paper is evenly spread on the mold.

12. Lay the mold onto the cloth and press down lightly to squeeze some of the water out onto the blotter. Continue this process until the all the water is squeezed from the pulp. Carefully pull the pulp away from the mold. Use a butter knife to release it. (Figure 6)

13. Lay the pulp on the blotter and carefully lift the left corner of the paper. Flip the federal seal over and slip it between the pulp and blotter. Press the pulp around the seal to make an impression. Use a pencil eraser or cotton swab to make more impressions and indentations. (Figure 7)

14. Sandwich a clean, dry cloth over the handmade paper. Do not move the presidential seal. Lay heavy books on top of it to give it weight. Change the blotting sheets periodically. (Figure 8)

15. Once the paper has dried, slowly peel it off the blotter cloth. Be careful not to damage the paper. Also, peel off the seal. (Figure 9)

16. Rough-out the Gettysburg Address in pencil onto the handmade paper. Do this before you attempt to use the crow-quill pen and India ink. Try a series of experiments to gain some experience writing in fancy scroll on the paper while using the pen and ink.

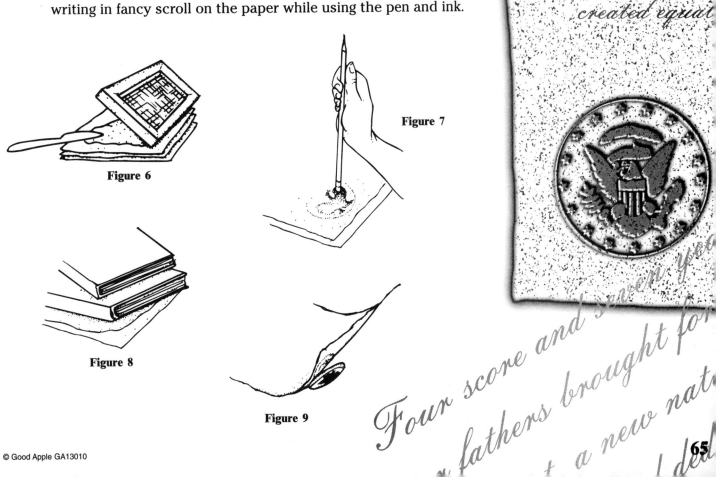

Figure 6

Figure 7

Figure 8

Figure 9

INDIVIDUAL PROJECT

Buttons, Belt Buckles, and Kepi Insignia Castings (Display)

Those soldiers who were lucky enough to wear the official uniforms of the Union and the Confederacy treasured their official brass buttons, insignias, and belt buckles. Many of the uniforms' buttons for both the North and the South were supplied by one company—the Waterburg Button Company, which is still in existence today. During the Civil War, the federal government bought the cast brass buttons directly from the company. The Confederate government was forced to buy their buttons through a British company that acted as the middleman for the Waterburg Button Company.

Figure 1

Materials

– polymer clay
– WD-40 oil or other cooking oil to use as a lubricant
– foam plate
– X-acto® knife

– sharp pencil or pen
– silicone adhesive
– brass-colored spray paint
– picture frame (optional)

Figure 2

Figure 3

Making the Die

1. Copy the design for the article you will be reproducing at 100%.

2. Trace the design onto the foam plate using a sharp pencil or pen. Make sure you press hard to make impressions you can see. (Figure 1)

3. Cut out the design using the X-acto® knife, then flip it over so it is backwards, and press into softened clay. This is the negative die form. (Figure 2)

4. Pull off the foam plate and form a wall of clay around the impressed design. Let dry. (Figure 3)

5. Spray the inside of the negative die with WD-40.

6. Press new, softened clay into the negative die form. Pull out and let dry. (Figure 4)

Figure 4

7. Spray the new impression with brass-colored paint. Make a series of buttons, buckles, and Kepi hat insignias to display in a frame. Glue them down with silicone adhesive. Try to keep the Union and Confederate designs in separate frames. (Figure 5)

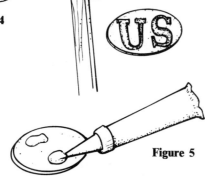

Figure 5

Official Insignias

Federal Seal

Confederate Seal

Federal Button

Confederate Button

Federal Belt Buckle

Kepi Insignia – Cavalry

Confederate Belt Buckle

Kepi Insignia – Artillery

Kepi Insignia – Infantry

FOR KIDS

Union Uniforms

Color the Union Army uniforms
by following the color key below.

1st Army of Tennessee (Cavalry)   19th Illinois Volunteers (Ellsworth Zouave Cadet)

Color Key

a. dark blue	c. yellow	e. black	g. brass
b. light blue	d. brown	f. red	

Union Cavalry Campsite Artifacts and Personal Affects

Color the Union Army campsite artifacts by following the color key below.

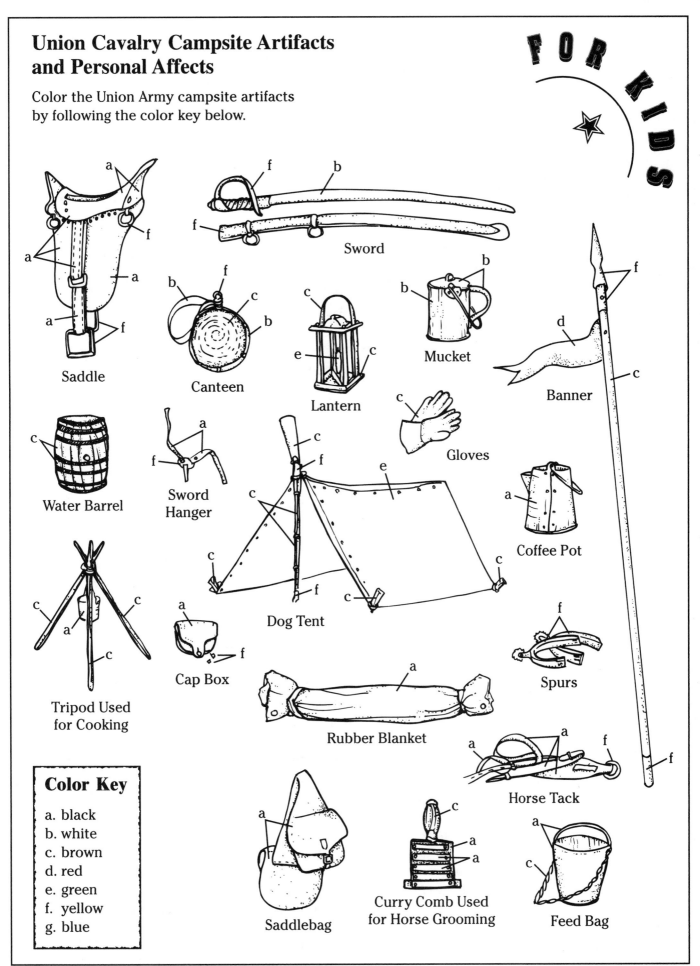

FOR KIDS

Saddle

Sword

Canteen

Lantern

Mucket

Banner

Gloves

Water Barrel

Sword Hanger

Coffee Pot

Dog Tent

Tripod Used for Cooking

Cap Box

Rubber Blanket

Spurs

Horse Tack

Color Key

a. black
b. white
c. brown
d. red
e. green
f. yellow
g. blue

Saddlebag

Curry Comb Used for Horse Grooming

Feed Bag

The wooden horse was one form of punishment to humiliate Union Soldiers who disobeyed orders, swore, were cowards, or were prone to drunkenness.

The End of the War (1864–1865)

BACKGROUND INFORMATION

The Civil War depleted every resource in the South and caused severe poverty for every citizen.

By this time, most Rebels went barefoot and wore rags, but they would not give in. Even under the worst circumstances, these troops held together by sheer desire, patriotism, and dedication to their beloved commanders.

In contrast, the northern economy flourished, but the morale of the people suffered. A great national bitterness emerged because of the North's constant losses and missed opportunities to end the war. Even the victory at Gettysburg was overshadowed by criticism toward General Meade for not pursuing the retreating Rebels. Furthermore, President Lincoln believed that if the Union did not win another major victory, he would lose the upcoming election for a second term in office and the desire to preserve the Union would be lost.

The Union Closes In

Lincoln was desperate for a strong commander, and in 1864 he named Ulysses S. Grant as Commander-in-Chief of all Union forces. General Grant had the reputation of being a fearless leader in the western campaign. As the commander, he devised a plan to disarm the Rebel Armies once and for all. Grant chose his strongest generals to carry out his orders, William T. Sherman and Philip Sheridan. General George Meade remained in charge of the Union army of the Potomac but under Grant's direction.

Most of the food and resources for the Confederate Army came from Virginia's fertile Shenandoah Valley. General Grant commanded General Sheridan and his Union cavalry to destroy all the granaries, farms, and livestock in the region. General Sherman was commanded to penetrate the deep South. It was believed that this action would deeply affect the Confederate morale. At the same time, General Grant was to move his forces across the Rapidan River and into Virginia. He planned to take Richmond once and for all to end the war.

In May 1864, Grant crossed the Rapidan River. He met Lee's Army of North Virginia in a heavily wooded area known as the Wilderness. After two days of fierce fighting, Lee was victorious. Unlike other Union generals, Grant was not intimidated.

After many major battles and constant fighting, Grant changed his tactics and moved his forces to Petersburg. This city lay 30 miles below Richmond. More importantly, Petersburg was a major rail station which supplied and transported Lee's army. Grant lay siege around the city by barricading his army in over 80 miles of trenches.

When Grant first crossed the Rapidan, General Sherman and his 62,000 soldiers marched into Georgia. There were continual battles against the Rebel General Joseph Johnston and the Army of Tennessee. Outnumbered with only 45,000 men, the Rebels held their ground. Still, General Sherman was determined to take Atlanta. He positioned his army around the city, and like Grant, lay siege.

At this time, the Rebel General Johnston was suddenly replaced by General John B. Hood. This new commander tried a series of attacks against the Union forces, but they failed miserably. In a desperate attempt to keep the Union out of Atlanta, General Hood moved his army away from the city and hoped the Union would follow. They did not, and Atlanta was taken on September 2, 1864.

The capture of Atlanta was the Union's military success of the year. It came just in time to ensure Lincoln's re-election. Two weeks after Atlanta fell, General Sherman demanded that every citizen leave their home, and fire was set to the entire city. In a further attempt to control the South, Sherman and his army "marched to the sea." They encountered little resistance and destroyed every farm, plantation, and city until they reached the Atlantic coast.

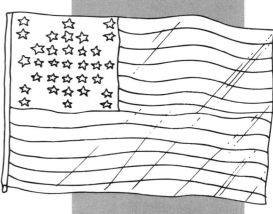

American Flag in 1865

General Lee Surrenders to General Grant

By February 1865, the Rebel Army was starving and worn out. General Lee was officially named Commander-in-Chief of all the Confederate forces. From what Lee could see, their future was bleak. Still, he refused to give up and attempted a series of brave attacks. But the Rebels could no longer hold their southern land nor protect their Richmond capital.

By April 3, the last drama of the war played itself out. Lee, and the remnants of his army, fled westward to once again find food. He planned to link up with the Army of the Tennessee, once again commanded by Johnston in Carolina. However, in an area of Virginia called Sayler's Creek, the Union overtook 6,000 retreating Rebel soldiers and forced their surrender. Grant urged Lee to give up the fight. "Not yet" was his answer.

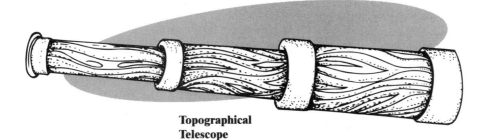

Topographical Telescope

On April 9, 1865, retreating Rebels wearily marched into the little town of Appomattox. Their route was cut off by the Union cavalry, led by General George Custer. As the Rebels pulled into formation for one last time, they discovered that the light screen of Union cavalry concealed a large mass of Union infantry.

This was enough for the exhausted Rebels to surrender their arms. In the early afternoon, Grant and Lee met in a home at Appomattox. Grant wrote the terms out which called for the immediate surrender of all Rebel arms. However, instead of retaining the men as prisoners of war, they were allowed to return home with the understanding that they pledge loyalty to the United States government. At Lee's request, Grant allowed the Rebel soldiers to keep their horses and mules. He also ordered food rations to feed the starving Rebels. General Lee believed that these terms were very generous and signed them. The Civil War had officially ended.

Surrender of Arms at Appomattox Court House

The Death of Lincoln

Less than a week after the surrender at Appomattox, President Lincoln could finally find comfort and relaxation. He and his wife went to Ford's Theatre to attend a popular play called *Our American Cousin*. At approximately 10:00 P.M., a deranged southern actor, John Wilkes Booth, sneaked into the president's box and fired a single bullet into the back of the president's head. On April 15, 1865 at 7:22 A.M., President Abraham Lincoln died. Both northerners and southerners mourned his loss.

☞ **F A C T**

★ ★ ★ ★ ★ ★ ★ ★ ★ ★ ★ ★ ★ ★

What is now Arlington National Cemetery was originally Confederate General Robert E. Lee's home. During the Civil War, the lack of grave sites caused the Federal forces to claim the land and the general's home and turn it into an army cemetery. This order was designated by the Union's Quarter-Master General Montgomery Meigs. Meigs was angry at Lee for becoming a Rebel and made sure that Lee and his family could never go back to their home.

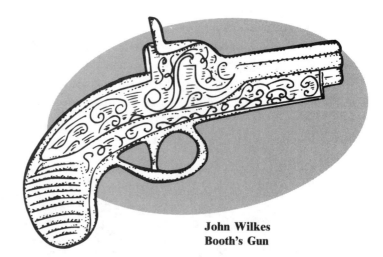

John Wilkes Booth's Gun

LEGEND

The Gentleman's Agreement

It was April 9, 1865 and General Lee stood rigid in the McLean House at Appomattox. He wore a crisp, gray uniform. An engraved sword was belted at his side. A fitting outfit, he thought, to wear while being taken as a prisoner. Then, the sound of galloping horses moved closer. He took a deep breath. Lee knew it was General Grant of the Union Army and he did not know what to expect.

General Grant stepped into the house. He looked at the great Confederate general, full of dignity and poise. Grant, the victor, felt embarrassed by his dirty private's shirt and mud-splattered uniform. To hide his own shame and to ease the tension of the moment, Grant began to speak of the time he first met Lee. After 25 minutes of talking about their days of fighting in the Mexican War, Lee suggested that they face the business at hand—the surrender of the Rebel troops. General Grant agreed, but how could he possibly ask such a great and respected man to surrender?

Grant put the terms of surrender on paper. They were very simple. These terms stated that Rebel officers and enlisted men were not to be held as prisoners of war but to be released on parole. The soldiers would have to give up their guns, but they could keep their knives and swords. Lee read the terms and commented, "These will have the best possible effect upon my men." Then, Lee asked if his men might keep their horses and mules so they could farm their land once they returned home. Grant agreed. Still concerned for his men, Lee mentioned that his men had not eaten for several days. General Grant immediately ordered 25,000 rations to feed the hungry Rebels.

In a war that was filled with so much division and bitter fighting amongst countrymen, the end was simple. The surrender was made with such dignity, respect, and integrity that it came to be known as the "Gentleman's Agreement."

GROUP PROJECT
Chess Set

Chess was a favorite pastime during the war. The strategies behind the game of chess are very much like how the generals operated against each other. War councils were brought together, and officers conferred with each other to develop carefully laid out strategies to draw their opponents into battles to win the war.

Materials

– wooden board or heavy cardboard, 11" x 11"
  (27.5 cm x 27.5 cm) square
– masking tape
– scissors
– ruler
– gray and blue flat latex or acrylic paint
– 1" (2.5-cm) paintbrush
– sponge
– plaster of Paris
– white glue
– 32 copper caps, 3/4" (2 cm) wide (found in hardware stores)

Making the Chess Men

1. For each side of a chess set there are 16 figures: one king, one queen, two bishops, two castles, two knights, and eight pawns. Enlarge the figures on page 77. You will need two copies for the front and back of each figure. Enlarge the figures so that their bases are all 1" (2.5 cm) wide. (Figure 1)

2. Color or paint each character in its appropriate colors—Union pieces blue, and Confederate pieces gray.

3. Glue each figure onto cardboard and cut out. Make sure to keep the rectangular form. Do the same thing to the backside of the cardboard. (Figure 2)

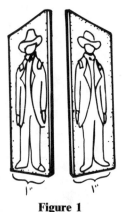

Figure 1

Figure 2

4. Take the copper cap and center it near the base. Identify where you need to make the slits so the figure will slip onto the cap. (Figure 3)

5. Pour plaster 3/4" (2 cm) deep into each copper cap. Slip the figure onto the cap and let the plaster set. Do this for each piece. (Figure 4)

Making the Board

6. Mark the borders of the board 1/2" (1.25 cm) all the way around. Mask out the borders and you should have a 10" (25-cm) square. Paint with one of the two colors and let dry. (Figure 5)

7. Mask off small, 1 1/4" (3-cm) squares to make eight squares down and across. Sponge in the opposite color paint from the base and lightly paint a textured pattern. Let dry and carefully pull off the tape. (Figure 6)

Figure 3   Figure 4

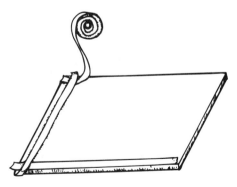

Figure 5   Figure 6

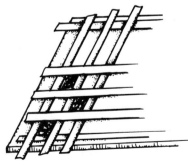

INDIVIDUAL PROJECT

Whittling (Soap or Wood)

Whittling was a favorite pastime with the soldiers from both sides. General Grant was particularly fond of whittling because it steadied his nerves during crucial battles. This was especially true when his troops were on the battlefield and their situation looked bleak.

Materials

- white soap bar
- plastic knife
- pencil
- soft wood, preferably balsa, sugar
  pine, willow, or northern white pine
  (the size of a soap bar)
- pen knife or carving tools

Before You Begin

Have students practice carving with the soap and plastic knife. Once they feel comfortable, they can advance to wood carving and follow the same procedure. Note that this project should not be attempted without parent or adult supervision. While using carving knives, always carve the wood with the tool positioned away from your body.

1. Draw the shape on both sides of wood. (Figure 1)

2. Slowly cut away by removing small chips. Try not to make big cuts. (Figure 2)

3. Gradually work down to your drawn shape. (Figure 3)

4. Roughly carve out the shape before you carve in details. (Figure 4)

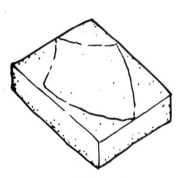

Figure 1

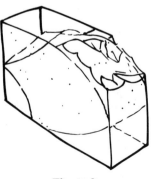

Figure 2

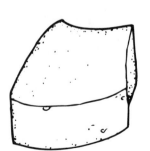

Figure 3

Figure 4

Chess Set Figures

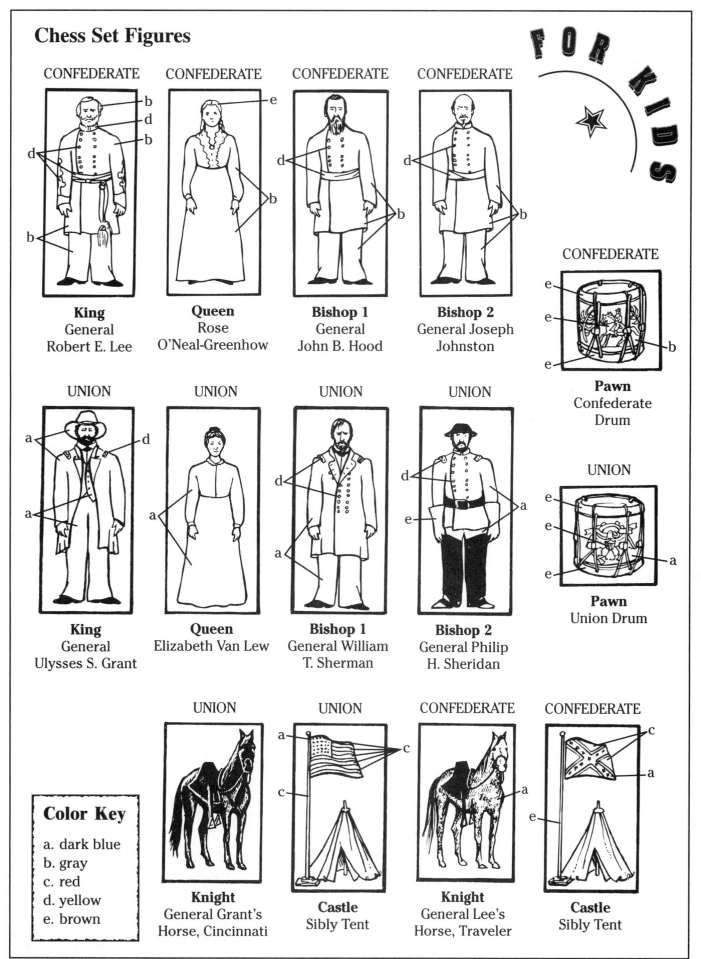

FOR KIDS

CONFEDERATE
King
General
Robert E. Lee

CONFEDERATE
Queen
Rose
O'Neal-Greenhow

CONFEDERATE
Bishop 1
General
John B. Hood

CONFEDERATE
Bishop 2
General Joseph
Johnston

CONFEDERATE
Pawn
Confederate
Drum

UNION
King
General
Ulysses S. Grant

UNION
Queen
Elizabeth Van Lew

UNION
Bishop 1
General William
T. Sherman

UNION
Bishop 2
General Philip
H. Sheridan

UNION
Pawn
Union Drum

UNION
Knight
General Grant's
Horse, Cincinnati

UNION
Castle
Sibly Tent

CONFEDERATE
Knight
General Lee's
Horse, Traveler

CONFEDERATE
Castle
Sibly Tent

Color Key

a. dark blue
b. gray
c. red
d. yellow
e. brown

Teacher's Note: Use this page as a flat coloring sheet or enlarge each item to use in one of the special projects described on pages 74 and 75.
© Good Apple GA13010

77

FOR KIDS

Generals Lee and Grant's Uniforms

Color the uniforms by following the color key below.

General Ulysses S. Grant (Union)

General Robert E. Lee (Confederate)

Color Key

a. dark blue	c. yellow	e. brown	g. brass
b. light blue	d. black	f. gray	h. white

Artifacts of General Grant, General Lee, and Appomattox Court House

Color the artifacts by following the color key below.

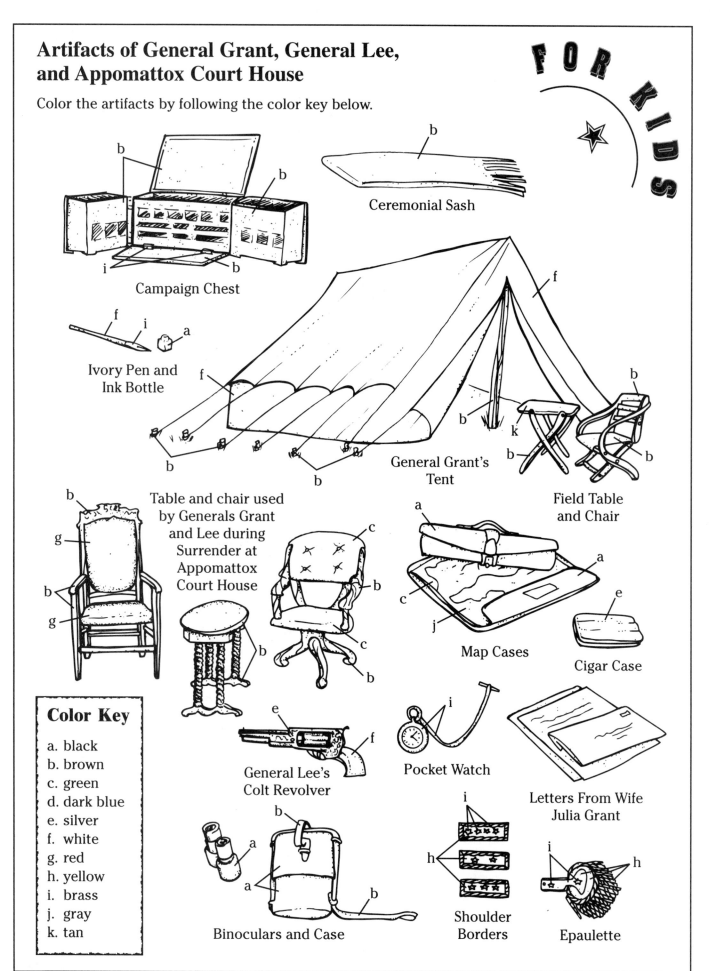

FOR KIDS

Campaign Chest

Ceremonial Sash

Ivory Pen and
Ink Bottle

General Grant's
Tent

Field Table
and Chair

Table and chair used
by Generals Grant
and Lee during
Surrender at
Appomattox
Court House

Map Cases

Cigar Case

General Lee's
Colt Revolver

Pocket Watch

Letters From Wife
Julia Grant

Binoculars and Case

Shoulder
Borders

Epaulette

Color Key

a. black
b. brown
c. green
d. dark blue
e. silver
f. white
g. red
h. yellow
i. brass
j. gray
k. tan

Bibliography

General Reference Books

Behind the Blue and Gray: The Soldiers' Life in the Civil War by Delia Ray (Puffin Books, 1991).

The Boys' War: Confederate and Union Soldiers Talk About the Civil War by Jim Murphy (Clarion Books, 1990).

Civil War: America Becomes One Nation—An Illustrated History for Young Readers by James I. Robertson (Knopf, 1996).

The Civil War: Strange and Fascinating Facts by Burke Davis (Holt, Reinhart, and Winston, 1982).

Cornerstones of Freedom: Fort Sumter by Brenda January (Children's Press, 1997).

Don't Know Much About the Civil War by Kenneth C. Davis (Avon, 1996).

Marching to Freedom: Blacks in the Civil War by James M. McPherson (Facts on File, 1991).

Photographic Views of Sherman's Campaign by George N. Barnard (Dover, 1977).

Sheridan's Ride by Thomas Buchanan Read (Greenwillow Books, 1993).

Sojourner Truth: Ain't I a Woman by Patricia McKissack (Scholastic, 1992).

Thunder at Gettysburg by Patricia Lee Gauch (Doubleday, 1975).

Till Victory is Won: Black Soldiers in the Civil War by Zak Mettger (Puffin, 1997).

Children's Literature

From Slave Ship to Freedom Road by Julius Lester (Dial Books, 1998).

If You Ever Lived at the Time of the Civil War by Kay Moore (Scholastic, 1994).

If You Ever Traveled on the Underground Railroad by Ellen Levine (Scholastic, 1988).

Minty: A Story of Young Harriet Tubman by Alan Schroder (Dial, 1996).

Rose in Bloom by Louisa May Alcott (Puffin Books, 1995).

Web Site Addresses

Abraham Lincoln Research Site —
> http://members.aol.com/RVSNorton/Lincoln2.html

Civil War Archive —
> http://civilwararchive.com

Civil War Collections from Gettysburg National Park —
> http://www.cr.nps.gov/csd/gettex

Civil War Photographs (Library of Congress) —
> http://lcweb2.loc.gov/ammem/cwphome.html

General Grant Web Site —
> http://ulysses@mscomm.com